W9-AUB-823

The
Custody Solutions
Sourcebook

WITHDRAWN

ALSO BY JANN BLACKSTONE-FORD:

My Parents Are Divorced, Too

WITHDRAWN

The
Custody Solutions
Sourcebook

by
Jann Blackstone-Ford

LOWELL HOUSE

LOS ANGELES

NTC/Contemporary Publishing Group

Library of Congress Cataloging-in-Publication Data

Blackstone-Ford, Jann.
    The custody solutions sourcebook / by Jann Blackstone-Ford.
        p.   cm.
    Includes bibliographical references and index.
    ISBN 0-7373-0075-2
    1. Custody of children—United States—Popular works. I. Title.
    KF547.Z9B58 1999
    346.7301'73—dc21   98-56041
                                                       CIP

Design by Mary Ballachino/Merrimac Design

Published by Lowell House
A division of NTC/Contemporary Publishing Group, Inc.
4255 West Touhy Avenue, Lincolnwood (Chicago), Illinois 60646-1975 U.S.A.
Copyright © 1999 by NTC/Contemporary Publishing Group, Inc.
All rights reserved. No part of this work may be reproduced, stored in a re-
trieval system, or transmitted or transmitted in any form or by any means,
electronic, mechanical, photocopying, recording, or otherwise, without prior
permission of NTC/Contemporary Publishing Group, Inc.
Printed in the United States of America
International Standard Book Number: 0-7373-0075-2
99 00 01 02 03 04 RRD 18 17 16 15 14 13 12 11 10 9 8 7 6 5 4 3 2 1

Contents

Foreword

Wander through any large bookstore and you will find volumes of books dedicated to every aspect of divorce, from separation to property settlement, but there is little information available that educates the divorcing parent about the custody of their children. As a practicing family law attorney and certified divorce and family mediator, I see divorcing couples struggle with child custody issues every day. They fear that not only must they suffer a horrible divorce but must also accept the child custody rules of years ago. The average person does not know that there are alternatives. Yes, they can accept a conventional custody agreement, but they can also legally design, in conjunction with their soon-to-be ex-spouse, a healthy living environment for their children after divorce.

Because of the ever-increasing number of divorces in America, there is a larger audience looking for alternative custody arrangements after separation. Not only are ex-wives with small children looking for better solutions for their children but also divorced fathers, single parents, and same-sex parents are seeking more creative ways to raise their children after divorce. Although I pride myself in my understanding of the law, I am unable to tell my clients how specific types of custody will work for them in their everyday lives. The logistics of joint custody, for example, may be different for parents who live in the same city as opposed to parents who live in different states. A parent who lives in the same city as their ex-spouse and has joint custody of their children may be expected to help with carpooling or to attend Little

League games. This is not possible when a parent does not live nearby, yet both sets of parents may have joint custody of their children.

Thank goodness a book like *The Custody Solutions Sourcebook* has finally been written. It explains in easy-to-understand language what can be expected from each type of custody alternative and offers suggestions from couples who have chosen that alternative. In their own words, they explain what worked, what didn't work, and why they chose a particular custody solution. Now parents can analyze all the information and decide what is indeed best for their family.

The goal of any parent is to create a healthy, happy life for their children. This becomes problematic when Mom lives in one house and Dad lives in another. Even so, hundreds of thousands of people across the country continue to raise children after divorce. As this lifestyle becomes more prevalent, the old rule of the kids live with Mom and visit Dad every other weekend just doesn't apply. *The Custody Solutions Sourcebook* helps the divorcing parent find creative custody alternatives, bearing no prejudice to the mother or the father of the child, only suggesting positive custody solutions to help parents raise happy children after divorce.

In *The Custody Solutions Sourcebook*, Jann Blackstone-Ford offers her personal experiences as a mother and stepmother as well as her experience as a divorce and family mediator and educator. Thus, *The Custody Solutions Sourcebook* is informative and entertaining, and I suggest it to anyone with children who is going through divorce.

—Barbara J. Kuehn

Preface

While doing research for my last book, *My Parents Are Divorced, Too*, I found a wealth of books on divorce, but very few that spoke directly to the emotional aspects of choosing one child custody alternative over another and then offering parents workable solutions. I am an educator and a divorce and family mediator, and I have been writing about blended family living, or the yours, mine, and ours concept, for ten years. It is my passion because it is my lifestyle. I have a daughter from a previous marriage, of whom I share custody with my ex-husband; two stepchildren; a daughter and a son, with whom my ex-husband shares joint physical custody with his ex-wife; and a daughter from this marriage. We are truly a yours, mine, and ours family.

The blending of our extended family has been a long process with some good days, some bad. I am happy to report that now there are far more good days than bad, but it has not always been so, so I understand the trials and tribulations of the divorce and blending process.

Child custody is the most complex and difficult issue divorcing parents face, and in times of anger and sadness, it is hard to put away our differences and make unselfish choices for our children. Fear and uncertainty can make negotiations with ex-spouses even more difficult. But with the divorce rates still hovering around 50 percent, and so many children produced from these severed unions, we, as parents, have to do something.

Perhaps a complete change in attitude toward divorce is needed. Granted, the ideal combination is a nuclear family, with a mother and a father living under the same roof, but the truth is that half of us cannot make our marriages work, and it is our children who are the true casualties of our custody wars.

So how can we fix this? If this were a true war between nations, after the fighting subsides, a détente would be called and negotiations made so that the warring nations could then coincide in peace. This rarely happens when a marriage ends. The opposing parties continue to fight even after the war is over. New problems arise and no problem-solving device is in place. Meanwhile, the children are left reeling from the discord around them.

We are lucky to live in a less rigid time, when we can design our own custody agreements to best support our children's needs. However, many divorcing couples do not know what is available to them. Many mothers fear that if they divorce, they will be left on their own to raise their children. Fathers often fear that if they divorce, they will never see their children again, or as one father I interviewed explained, "I see them so little, why bother?" There are alternatives to these extremes, and this book is designed to help you find the custody solution that is correct for your family.

The Custody Solutions Sourcebook takes you through all the custody alternatives legally available in a logical progression so that you understand each alternative and can make a well-informed decision for your family. The solutions offered are compiled from my lectures on blended family living and interviews with hundreds of couples facing the decision of how to raise their children after divorce. Some of the suggestions may seem unconventional, some may seem too logical if you are in the middle of a divorce and still angry at your spouse, but these solutions have worked for parents just like you, which is why they have been included in this book.

The common thread running through *The Custody Solutions Sourcebook* is the idea of setting aside your differences—whatever they may be—and putting your children first. Some have scoffed when I have suggested this, saying that if parents really put their children first, they would have never divorced in the first place. While today "irreconcilable differences" do make it easy to get a divorce, professionals no longer suggest that battling spouses stay together for the sake of the children. The question we must ask ourselves as parents is: Is it better to remove yourself from a bad situation and then teach your children a positive way to deal with occasional conflict, or should you continue to live in a bad relationship, where conflict is commonplace, stress abides, and the emotional stability of each family member is in question?

The answer, of course, is a personal decision, and will continue to be debated by parents and professionals. But if we do decide to divorce, it is still our responsibility as parents to give our children a happy life—which brings us to the reason *The Custody Solutions Sourcebook* was written.

Chapter one, "Examining Divorce: What Does It Really Mean to You and Your Children?" begins by discussing divorce and then offers a realistic look at what it means to both you and your kids. It explains how to tell the kids once you have decided to divorce, examines a child's attitude about divorce so you can be prepared for resulting behaviors, and also offers tips for ethical behavior between spouses during the divorce process and afterward, when reality sets in.

Chapter two, "Where to Begin?" explores your rights as a parent and answers legal questions about the custody of your children. Chapter two's message is to *educate yourself*. Even if you choose to use an attorney to represent you in court, you should have a good idea of what you want for your children after the divorce. An attorney, or judge for that matter, does not know that Billy worships his father, and to comfort him after your separation he needs to see his dad more than every other weekend. An attorney or judge does not know that little Lisa is still breastfeeding and cannot be away from her mother for more than a few hours. Granted, perhaps the best way to cope with the latter problem is to change to bottle-feeding, but these are the types of decisions that should be made by the parents, not the courts.

It is important to mention that *The Custody Solutions Sourcebook* is not a law book. Although I state the direction that laws may slant in a given situation, I am not a lawyer and cannot predict how a judge will respond. The text has been reviewed by numerous attorneys, but like all laws, current custody laws regularly change. It should also be noted that custody laws differ from state to state. What is legal in California may not be legal in New Hampshire. I have tried my best to offer general information, but before you file any paperwork, check with an attorney or a legal aid society to see if what you propose is legal within your state.

Chapters three through six explain, via stories I have compiled from interviewing hundreds of couples over the years, the different types of custody alternatives available including sole custody, joint custody, joint physical custody, and bird's nest custody. Most of the names and cities have been changed to protect the privacy of the couples supplying the stories, but I can assure you that they are all true. At the end of each chapter I have established a parent panel from the parents interviewed and have asked them some poignant questions. They will explain firsthand how their custody agreements work, why they chose the solution they did, how it affected their children, and if they would make the same decisions again.

Chapter seven is dedicated to exploring the perplexing question of same-sex parenting and custody. Since there are no formal laws recognizing gay and lesbian couples, many of these questions are answered from a single parent standpoint. You will also find answers to custody questions specific to single mothers and fathers.

Child support issues are discussed in chapter eight. Common questions about child support payment, collection, and modification are addressed.

In the second to last chapter, "A Step-by-Step Guide to Creating Your Own Custody Solution," we hear from parents who have designed their own custody solution and how they used bits and pieces of the different conventional custody alternatives to mold an agreement of their own. What this really means is that they were able to go with the flow and make changes when problems arose. No one deviated so far from the norm that you could not put yourself in their place and imagine what it was like for them. You will learn how parents decided upon a specific agreement, and, if their original idea didn't work, how they made the appropriate changes.

By the end of this book you will be custody-aware, so the last chapter, "Getting Along and Making Your Custody Solution Work," offers suggestions on how to get along after divorce—not just with your ex but with your new spouse's ex, as well. Chapter ten includes stories from couples who have worked to make a success of their divorce, and also examines divorce through the eyes of the children it affects. I have even included some of my own stories to explain the progression I went through while struggling to be a better parent and stepparent.

It is my sincere desire that this book helps us all raise healthy, well-adjusted children after divorce, and I sincerely thank each person I interviewed for their patience and contribution to making this book a reality.

Acknowledgments

When I began to write this book, I asked for solutions from other divorced parents via my website www.custodysolutions.com. I had no idea I would get such a response! Because of the wonder of computer networking, I now have some friends that I have never met, but I need to acknowledge for their sincere stories and custody solutions. I know them only by their e-mail addresses, but let me now say thank you.

My thanks to George Thomas for his help on the legal issues, Barbara Kuehn for her foreword, and Sally Elkington and Kate Kendell for their updates on same-sex marriage and parenting. Special thanks to everyone at Lowell House for their patience and for allowing me the extra time I needed.

I would also like to thank my wonderful blended family for their patience while I compiled the information for this book, especially my husband, Larry. And to my daughter, Annie. Honey, *this* is what I do for a living.

"*The entire legal profession, lawyers, judges, law school teachers, has become so mesmerized with the stimulation of the courtroom contest that we tend to forget that we should be healers of conflict. For many claims, trial by adversarial contest must in time go the way of the ancient trial by battle and blood. Our system is too costly, too painful, too destructive for a truly civilized people.*"
—FORMER CHIEF JUSTICE WARREN BURGER,
1984 State of the Judiciary Address

CHAPTER ONE

Examining Divorce:
What Does It Really Mean To You and Your Children?

> *"When written in Chinese, the word 'crisis' is composed of two characters—one represents danger, and the other represents opportunity."*
>
> —JOHN F. KENNEDY, 1959,
> quoting Saul David Alinsky

We have all heard the statistics—50 percent of all marriages in the United States end in divorce. But don't we think we will be the ones to make it? We will weather the storm for better or worse. Then one day, much to our surprise, we find we are *the* 50 percent, the 50 percent who do divorce, and our lives, and the lives of our children, are turned upside down.

How Did We Get Here?

My father-in-law and I are collaborating on yet another book, and because of this, we have lengthy conversations on a variety of subjects. According to him, I seem to be a reasonable human being, so he found it odd that I had been married before and then divorced. To his way of thinking, reasonable human beings don't get a divorce. To people of his generation, if you divorce, it means there's something wrong with you. If you can't make a marriage work, you are flawed in some way, and since he has known me since I was young and could discern no obvious flaws, he felt compelled to ask me why my ex-husband and I divorced. *What was wrong with me?*

Understanding that I have been happily married to his son for the last ten years, at first I felt uncomfortable with his question. I hadn't thought about the reasons for my divorce in quite a while, and in order to answer my father-in-law honestly I had to reconstruct in my mind some of the old situations before I could respond with what I thought was the reason for my separation. As I spoke, I was surprised to hear what I said. It was nothing like the reasons I quoted right after my divorce. I now had greater insight into the person my ex-husband had become and into the person I used to be, so I spoke of much deeper conflicts than "he was angry all the time" or "he wasn't nice to me," which were the reasons I used to spout whenever asked. I came away with an entirely new perception of why my ex-husband and I divorced, and it all boiled down to a lack of communication—not for the lack of trying, just an inability to talk to each other.

A Child's Perception

I ended our conversation by expressing my concern for my daughter from my first marriage and how the divorce had affected her. As difficult as it was for me to accept a separation, it was far more devastating for her to understand the changes that were imposed on her when her father and I no longer lived together. I realized that divorce affects every aspect of a child's life. It severs their security, and as a result they may feel disoriented, abandoned, even depressed at times. As parents, we may not even notice the transformation. Our children look fine. They do not appear to be sullen or withdrawn; there are no obvious signs that something is wrong. But suddenly your son begins to act out at school, or your daughter begins to have nightmares. This could happen months after the initial separation, so it may not be obvious that it's the divorce that is directly affecting your children. Bottom line? If you're fighting a roller coaster of emotions, your kids are too.

A child's perception of divorce depends on how old they are at the time of separation. Each child reacts differently. Some become depressed, some manifest symptoms of anxiety, some seem to float through the crisis as if there were nothing wrong. There is not even a guarantee that two siblings will respond the same to their parents' divorce. Children younger than four seem to grasp bits and pieces of the discord around them but are unable to articulate what they feel. Older children often react with misdirected anger. In other words, they know they are angry, but they are not sure why.

Bill, an eleven-year-old sixth grader, began a ritual of kicking his desk before he sat down in class. It was obvious he was angry, but when questioned by his teacher, he had no answers. His teacher informed Bill's parents that he was having outbursts of anger for no apparent reason. She saw a previously happy and well-behaved boy now manifesting his anger physically, and she was concerned this behavior might advance into fistfights with other students. When Bill's parents informed her that Bill's father had moved out of the family home a week before, the teacher understood the correlation.

Jessica had just turned five, but the joy of starting kindergarten was overshadowed by the fact that her father had recently moved out of her house. Each morning Jessica's mother would make her a lunch and drive her to school. About an hour into the school day, Jessica would have a severe stomachache and want to go home. After the fourth consecutive day of Jessica coming home early, Jessica's mother decided it was time to take her to the doctor. Of course, nothing was medically wrong with the child. The school counselor, trained in child psychology, was consulted, and Jessica was diagnosed as suffering from anxiety. The stomachaches were brought on by her parents' separation.

Anxiety and anxiety-related illnesses like Jessica's stomachaches are a common response to divorce. Be on the lookout for excessive worry, sadness, depression, or mood swings in children who are normally even-tempered. Fear of being left alone or fear of leaving you is another common response in children of divorce. Beware if a normally independent child who loves to spend the night at friends' homes becomes clingy and chooses to stay home and watch TV with you. At first, you may feel complimented, but if this behavior goes on too long, this change may signal that your child is suffering from anxiety. Studies have shown that if conflict can be kept to a minimum, children have a better chance of coping with the anxiety divorce creates.

Fighting May Not Be Enough

Most children will acknowledge that when their parents fight, it makes them unhappy, and they want them to stop. If there has been violence or abuse, they want that to stop, too, but child psychologists report that children may not see fighting and unhappiness as a good enough reason for parents to divorce. Although spouses see the divorce as the solution to their problems, children view it as the problem itself. Most kids are willing to forgive and forget in hopes that their forgiveness will prevent a permanent separation.

A case in point: When Martin and Rachel, a couple from New Mexico, told their children of their impending separation, they were surprised by their reaction.

"My children are older," explains Rachel. "Sam is thirteen, and Shannon is fifteen. We thought it was obvious to them how unhappy we were. We fought all the time. They saw it, but when we told them we were getting a divorce, they acted like it was all a big surprise."

Children hear the word *divorce* but often don't understand what it means to their life. My own stepdaughter, Melanie, explained to me that at the age of four, when her parents separated, her mother gently informed her of the impending divorce. But when her father moved out, she was still confused.

"I knew about divorce. Some of my friends' parents were divorced. But when it happened in my life I just thought that meant the fighting would stop. At four I didn't understand that divorce meant Daddy wouldn't live with us anymore. It was a shock when he walked out the door," explains Melanie.

Wishful Thinking

It is not uncommon for children to wish secretly that their parents would reconcile. It also doesn't seem to matter how long their parents have been apart for Mommy and Daddy to be back together again.

By the time my stepdaughter, Melanie, was nine years old, her parents had been divorced for almost four years. I will never forget the time she and I were cuddled up on the bed, watching television. "Janny," she asked out of the blue, "do you think my parents will get back together?" I was taken aback. I had been happily married to her father for two years.

As surprised as I was by Melanie's question, it was obvious that she had been hoping for a reconciliation for a long time; she just never mentioned it to anyone. It was true that she and I had formed a strong bond in our two years as a family, but no matter how content Mel was with our new arrangement, it appeared that her sincerest wish was for it to be the way it used to be. And this was something her father and I could not give her.

I responded with, "Oh, honey, I don't think that will happen. Daddy and I are married now, but your mommy and daddy both love you very much . . . and you know I do, too." She cuddled up a little closer and whispered, "I know."

And that was the end of it, until she was sixteen and we were discussing that very conversation. She laughed at the idea that she had asked her father's new wife if she thought her parents would ever reconcile. "What was I thinking?" Melanie offered. To me, it didn't seem that complicated. She was thinking plain and simple—without all the adult complications—she wanted her mom and dad to still be married.

I have used this story in my lectures about children and their reactions to divorce as an example of a child's private longing for her parents to reconcile, and the response from the audience has been mixed. Some see the irony in Melanie's comment, and I hear a resounding "ahhhh" from the audience. Others, who have a more volatile relationship with their stepchildren, regard her comment as fuel for an argument. "She was just trying to get at you," one women said when the lecture was opened to questions and comments. That may have been her experience, but in my case I knew Melanie had no ulterior motives. She was not telling me she did not like me or that she wished I was not in her life. We were cuddling while watching TV at the time of her question.

At that moment I wasn't her father's wife or her stepmom. I was a trusted friend in whom she could secretly confide her private thoughts. I was grateful for the confidence.

"How should we tell the kids?"

Key word? *We.* If possible, it is best that you and your spouse are together when you present to your children your plans to divorce. This way, you will appear to be of the same mind and you will both be on hand if questions arise. If you absolutely cannot be in the same room with your soon-to-be ex-spouse, agree together what you will say to the kids, and then stick to it. Don't deviate from your original plan or talk behind your spouse's back. This behavior will backfire on you. Your kids love you both, and even if you feel you are more correct or more hurt than your spouse, your animosity will only further confuse your children.

"What do we say?"

"My husband traveled on business, so when we separated, it was not obvious to my son, Spencer, that his father and I were getting a divorce," recalls Eileen Mendoza. "Unfortunately, other adults in the neighborhood knew before I got the courage to say anything to Spencer, and they discussed it with their children. Then, one day, Spencer came home crying after a play date because his friend asked how he felt now that his parents were getting a divorce. It was a shock to him. I wished I had handled it differently."

The first step to presenting divorce as a solution to your family problems is to be sure the divorce is inevitable. Although many couples make it a practice not to fight in front of the children, sometimes an argument pops up and parents are too overwhelmed to stop, even if their children are nearby. Casually mentioning separation in front of your children frightens them and causes them to worry about something beyond their control. If divorce is not truly an option, don't bring it up. They are affected each time you mention it in front of your children.

If you have exhausted all avenues of reconciliation and have decided that divorce is truly the correct course of action, *before* you talk to them decide where your children will live, and have a proposed visitation schedule for both parents. Let them know that you are in control and they can turn to you if they are confused. When asked, "Where are we going to live?" your reply should be concise and to the point. Saying things like, "Gee, honey, we really don't know exactly where we are going to live. Daddy and Mommy just wanted you to know what is going on" does not make your children feel secure. Instead, try, "Mom will stay in this house, and Dad will move only two miles away. We both love you very much."

"The next question will inevitably be: 'Why?'"

Have an answer prepared. Remember, if possible, your spouse is sitting next to you, so don't say something that would inevitably cause another fight or paint your spouse in a poor light. Granted, your husband may have run off with another woman or your wife may have a drug problem, but your kids don't need to know the intimate details the minute they are told their family is splitting up. Instead, they need to know what is in store for them. They must be reassured how *you feel about them*. They must feel secure in this time of uncertainty and upheaval.

The true "why" answer is a personal one, and some parents may not know what to say to their children when asked. "Make your explanation age-appropriate," suggests Dr. Steve Asrican, a psychologist practicing in the Boston area. "A five-year-old may not understand that Mommy has been irritable for the last few years because of a drug problem, but a fifteen-year-old will understand and should know that the reason his parent is not living at home is because they are in rehab. Not only because the child is old enough to understand the situation, but because at fifteen they should be made aware of the dangers of drugs. They have seen their parent's deterioration firsthand." Asrican adds, "I am not suggesting you lie to your younger child, but using the word *hospital* rather than *drug rehabilitation center* may be a better choice."

Think carefully about what you will say. A young mother from Dallas once told me how she explained to her five- and six-year-old children that she and their father were divorcing. "When Dakota asked me why we were getting a divorce, I was so angry and hurt I just said, 'Because your father ran off with another woman, that's why.' Not thinking it would sink in, two days later I overheard Dakota discussing the separation with his little friend. He used the exact words I had used: His father 'had ran off with another woman, that's why.' I was so ashamed that I'd let my anger interfere with my reason that I asked his friend to go home so I could better explain things to Dakota—in a way that he could understand."

Asrican suggests there are many ways to explain a breakup so as not to undermine either parent in the eyes of their children. "I speak as a professional and as a divorced father. When children ask why you are getting a divorce, they may not want to know the exact reason as much as they need reassurance that both parents still love *them* even though there will be big changes ahead. So, when asked, try to steer clear of blaming your ex-spouse for the breakup. Blame in an explanation only justifies your position in your own mind. It will not help your children cope with the divorce. It will only further estrange parent from child."

Here's an example of a good way to start talking to your children about your inevitable divorce: "You may have noticed Mom and Dad are fighting a lot. We don't get along as well as we used to. We have talked about it and we feel it would be better to live apart."

If your children see you sitting together while you are calmly telling them that you plan to separate, they may say, "But you're not fighting now, why do you have to get a divorce?"

This is a complicated but valid question. Now you can explain that you are both calm because you have made the decision, and you are both comfortable with it.

Be careful. Most children have an idea that divorce means the end of something. They may not understand exactly what, but love is in there somewhere. Younger children do not understand the difference between love for your spouse and love for them. A child may conclude that if you get a divorce and no longer love each other, your love for them may also end. This would be a good time to explain that although you do not get along with your spouse, that does not mean you both don't love your children. Reassure them that *your love for them* will never change.

"Is it my fault?"

Countless studies on divorce show that children often blame themselves for their parents' divorce. They feel in some way that they caused the breakup. If only they were better, smarter, or prettier children, Mommy and Daddy wouldn't get a divorce.

"I knew my parents were going to get a divorce," says James, a teenager from St. Petersburg, Florida. "There wasn't a lot of fighting in front of me, but I could just feel it in my bones. I remember thinking, 'I'll go home and clean my room and do everything my parents tell me to do and they won't split up.' When I found out they were getting a divorce even though I was good, I felt even more helpless."

Lorus, a twenty-year-old first-year college student from West Virginia, reiterates James's feelings, but her reaction was even more extreme. "I was sixteen when my parents divorced. I was on the honor roll, in college-prep classes, well on my way toward my career goal of someday practicing law. Then, *pow*, my parents announced they were getting a divorce and I went straight downhill. It didn't matter how good I was, or how much I achieved, they were still getting a divorce and the world seemed futile. Slowly, school became less important. I was so depressed I started taking drugs, and that was it. I was on a roller coaster for a year and a half. I'm twenty and finally entering college, but it has taken a lot of time with my counselor to help me realize my parents' divorce had nothing to do with me. Even today I get little pangs of, maybe if I had graduated early and gone off to college sooner, my parents might still be together. Intellectually, I know their divorce wasn't my fault, but in my heart, sometimes I still think there must have been something I could have done to prevent it."

"No one can anticipate how their children will react to their news of divorce," explains Asrican. "Even though you think you have covered all the bases, you may not have. My advice is to count to ten when dealing with your ex-spouse. Paint him in the most positive light with which you feel comfortable, and stay available to your children for questions, because if your kids feel that questions they may ask will make you angry, they won't ask them, which only perpetuates their confusion."

As parents, we know that our children did not cause our divorce, but our children may not be so sure. Whatever the reason, the decision to divorce is our responsibility and ours alone. During your conversation with your children, it is imperative that both you and your spouse are careful to reiterate that ending your marriage is your choice and not the fault of your children.

"What truly changes when you get a divorce?"

Partners often believe that when their divorce is final, their ex-spouse will finally be out of their life. But if you are conscientious parents, nothing is further from the truth. Divorce may end your marriage, but if you have children, your relationship with your ex-spouse never ends. Even if you no longer live together you must still make decisions together for the welfare of your children. You will still see each other on a regular basis—at Little League games, school plays, or at open house at your child's school, no matter your custody agreement.

Each divorce is different, but some changes are inevitable. First, for both parents, the time you spend with your children becomes quality time. Depending on the custody agreement you choose (we will discuss the custody alternatives available to you in chapter three), the days you spend with your children will be fewer because you are now splitting your child's time between two parents. It can be difficult for parents to grasp that *both* parents have the right to spend time with their children after divorce. You may feel that your ex-spouse is just upsetting things by wanting extra time with *your* kids, but it is more likely she misses them just as much as you do, and she also craves some order after the disruption of divorce.

Second, your household expenses will increase. You are now maintaining two households, so your cost of living will probably rise. That's why both parents may have to work outside the home, which means further disruption for children whose mother did not work outside the home before the divorce. Current statistics show that the average U.S. marriage lasts a little longer than seven years. Therefore, most children of divorce are younger than seven at the time of separation, so you should anticipate an additional expense for child care.

Your children are not only experiencing a new life, but also a new *lifestyle*. Because money may be less available than before the divorce, it is best to prepare them by having a frank discussion of what they can expect. In my own home after my divorce, my daughter and I had a "heart-to-heart" that included a discussion of which extracurricular activities were still affordable. When my daughter's father and I lived together, we spent every Friday evening eating dinner out and attending a movie. Now that we were divorced and I had primary custody of my daughter, I could not afford the extra cost of dinner and a movie once a week, and she missed her "movie night." We decided to turn movie night into an event at home. My daughter and a friend could choose a video from the local rental store. We then bought all the makings for *s'mores*, a marshmallow-chocolate concoction between graham crackers, and ate them in front of the television. We speared the marshmallows on long barbecue forks and roasted them in the fireplace while we watched the movie. My daughter thought this was great fun, and it cost a fraction of what dinner and a movie would! Divorce can make you become quite inventive!

Third, your attitude toward each other changes. Moving from a two-parent to a one-parent household is not an easy transition for parent or child. Both spouses now view themselves as a separate entity, the head of their household, and making decisions for your children can become more difficult because each parent believes they are the boss. The truth is, both parents are. Instead of just one family, your children now have two, both equal, and hopefully, both positive nurturing environments.

Not only does your attitude toward each other change, but the way your children view the two of you will also change. You are no longer Mom *and* Dad, but Mom *or* Dad. I have always found this realization sad but necessary to accept if your family is to move toward healing and resuming a "normal" life.

The Ten Rules of Ethical Behavior

Everything changes after divorce and no matter how you anticipate these changes, new issues will crop up, each of which demands fair judgment and creativity. The following ten tips are suggestions, or rules of behavior, to guide divorcing parents through their new life together beyond divorce. They are rules that everyone knows but in the heat of anger often forgets. They are ethical rules that ask you to treat your ex-spouse as you would like to be treated. They ask you to put your children ahead of the problem, as well as base your decisions on your love for them. As a matter of fact, that's the primary and first rule of ethical behavior after a divorce.

1. Always Put Your Children First

Before you say or do anything mean or vindictive, look at your children. Think about how your comment or action will impact them, and then act accordingly. Don't use your children as pawns to get back at your ex-spouse. If you want revenge, perhaps the sweetest is to pick yourself up, dust yourself off, and make a success of your new, unmarried life. Teaching your children to meet adversity head-on is a far better lesson than dragging them through the mud of divorce, which does not show them how to cope in the future should they have a similar problem. Your children can go to counseling for years, but how you handle your divorce in front of them will be ingrained in their minds forever.

2. Keep Your Anger to Yourself

If you are angry at your ex-spouse, if he says something over the phone or in person that makes you crazy, keep it from your kids. This may seem like a perfect time to look at little Susie, and say, "That father of yours is such a jerk. He ran off with that bimbo and he deserves everything he gets!" Don't do it. Keep your anger to yourself. When you say something offensive about your ex-wife or ex-husband to one of your children, you are saying something offensive about your child's mother or father. It could backfire, as in the case of Annie, a bright fourteen-year-old whose parents recently divorced.

"I used to hate to go see my dad because he was always making snide remarks about my mom. It was obvious he didn't approve of her choices. He didn't like where she lived or her lifestyle. He never came out and said it. It was just obvious by the tone in his voice when he spoke about her. It made me very uncomfortable, and I didn't want to be there. I wanted to stop going to his house on weekends."

What do you do in a case like this? If the ex-wife calls her ex-husband and complains, will it make any difference? They didn't get along when they were married, why would the ex-husband stop this behavior after they were divorced? "The ex-wife must explain to her ex-husband that his comments are hurting their child, not her, and his behavior is affecting their father/daughter relationship," explains Asrican. Understanding that, Annie's father stopped berating her mother in front of her. Although the parents' relationship did not improve, the problems were not flaunted in front of their child.

3. Never Ask a Child to Choose With Which Parent They Want to Live

Children love both parents equally. Even though it may not be your intention, the fact that you are divorcing puts your child in the middle. And to complicate matters, if a child is asked with which parent they want to live, they are in essence being asked to choose one parent over the other. Your child is already reeling from the divorce. The added pressure of choosing sides only reinforces his insecurity and undermines his positive readjustment.

When Susan and Joe Fitzgerald divorced, they agreed upon joint physical custody of their children, Pami, age four, and Vincent, age eight (see chapter five, joint physical custody). Pami and Vincent seemed so upset when it was time to leave Susan's home and go to their father's that Susan tried to reassure her children by telling them they could choose with whom they wanted to live when they turned fourteen. Susan had been an assistant in a divorce attorney's office some years before and, thinking she understood custody law, felt comfortable making that statement.

Susan's comment that her kids could eventually pick where they wanted to live seemed innocent, but it is a misstatement for a number of reasons.

First, when examined in counseling, Susan admitted the comment was said not only to appease the children but to subconsciously undermine her ex-husband's authority in her children's eyes. Susan never wanted the 50/50 division of her children's time that joint custody offered. She wanted them to live with her all the time. Her ex-husband, a devoted father, fought for the 50/50 joint physical custody agreement and was very happy with the arrangement. This made Susan furious.

Second, Pami and Vincent didn't necessarily want to live with their mother all the time. Their request to not leave her home was in response to her behavior each time they packed up to go to their father's home. Susan cried. Her children, not wanting to hurt their mother's feelings, tried to make her feel better by telling her they didn't want to leave.

Third, as children of divorce grow older, many opt to live with the other parent, but if the child is small when the parents divorce and custody has already been decided by the court, the decision is not simply overturned when the child becomes a teenager, as Susan implied. Most judges feel an older child can successfully articulate where they want to live. If the child is thirteen or fourteen at the time of divorce, the court usually takes the child's wishes into consideration when deciding placement.

"What Susan's statement did in reality," Asrican notes, "was extend her children's period of readjustment after the divorce.

Subconsciously, the children felt they may eventually have to move, and the room they liked or the couch on which they did their homework would again change. Plus, in the back of their minds, they knew that if they did choose, they would have to hurt one of their parents—something no child wants to do."

4. Ask Your Ex-Spouse If You Have a Question

Bobby, a lively nine-year-old, returned to his mother's house after visiting his father for the weekend. Normally, upon leaving his father's house he was animated and talkative. This time, he did not want to go back. It was hard for a nine-year-old to put his reasons into words, but when coaxed, he explained that he felt like he was in trouble whenever he visited his dad. It seemed that on each visit his father would sit him down and ask him questions about his mother. Did she have a boyfriend? Did the boyfriend ever sleep over? Was that a new car I saw her driving? Bobby felt that he was being interrogated by the police and grew afraid of his father's questions. "I thought maybe Mom was doing something wrong. I didn't know. Dad seemed so mad," he says.

As it was, Bobby's mother's did have a new boyfriend. He did occasionally sleep over, but not when Bobby was at home, so Bobby could not give his father an accurate account of his mother's new relationship. Yes, his mother was driving a new car, but Bobby did not know enough about his mother's job to explain that his mother had just gotten a promotion and the car was paid for by her company.

Don't assume your children know the correct answers. If you are curious about something, ask your ex-spouse, not your children. Pressure on your children from too many questions will cause stress that can manifest as behavioral problems, sleep disorders, or poor schoolwork.

5. Be Fair

Rules change as you adjust to your new life. Children get older, a parent moves or gets a new job, old problems are solved and new problems rear their ugly heads. If you want a favor, think, "Would I grant this favor if she asked me?" If the answer is no, perhaps you should reevaluate the question. Be Fair. Don't ask your ex-spouse to do anything you are not willing to do, and the favor will eventually be returned.

6. Act As If You Are in Control

You do not have to be domineering or unwilling to listen when a disagreement with your ex arises. Being in control means you give your children the impression that you are comfortable with your decisions, and everything is fine. Make sure they understand that their parents are taking care of them. If your children feel you are confused, they will not feel grounded. The goal is to make the transition from marriage to divorce easy for them.

Younger children feel most comfortable when they think their parents have taken care of all the custody decisions: where they will live, with whom, when, etc. Older children, however, may become resentful if all decisions are made for them. Teenagers need to know that their wishes are being considered, but they must also understand the ultimate custody decision lies with their parents and the courts.

7. Be Their Parent

It is not uncommon in times of stress to need a confidant, someone to lean on. If, during your divorce, this role falls to your children, confiding your innermost secrets may translate into insecurity for them. "Yipes! Mom or Dad doesn't know what they are doing, either!"

If you need someone to talk to about adult decisions, for example, should you date someone new, should you allow them to sleep over, should you blow the life savings on plastic surgery, or should you invest in a particular stock, consider talking to a therapist, an investment counselor, maybe a plastic surgeon . . . not your children.

8. Don't Let Your Guilt Allow You to Make Bad Decisions

Parents harbor enormous guilt about divorce. They perceive that a decision for which they are responsible has turned their child's world upside down. This guilt often clouds their decision-making process; perhaps they overcompensate by saying yes when they should say no.

"Dad, can I spend the night at Lisa's?" asked Sarah, a ten-year-old becoming accustomed to the changes of living in two households. This was a difficult question for Sarah's father. He wanted to make his daughter happy. She had been through so much recently, but *tonight* was a school night. When Sarah's parents were together the rule was no sleeping over on school nights. Sarah's dad now lived alone after the divorce, so he could override this rule and finally make Sarah happy. Such a decision would alleviate his own guilt, but it might not be the best choice for Sarah.

"I gritted my teeth and said, 'Sorry, Sarah. Not on a school night.' Inwardly I recognized I was taking the first step toward getting back a normal life after the divorce. I explained that because her mother and I were divorced did not mean that the rules had changed. She continued to push, but she eventually understood," he recalls.

9. Appear as a United Front

The preceding story continued. Sarah's next comment to her father was, "But Mom lets me." Sarah's father felt his anger toward his ex-spouse rise until he realized he was being manipulated. Children figure out how to overcome an anticipated "no!" when parents live together. Living apart is fertile ground for manipulation, because neither parent wants to appear to be the "bad guy." Coordinating disciplinary tactics is difficult. It can become even more difficult if discipline was a source of irritation while the family lived under one roof.

"Really?" asked Sarah's father. "Let's call her." Sarah knew that she had been caught. Sarah's mother and father had both agreed that the rules would stay the same, even if they were divorced.

"No, that's okay," said Sarah. "I have homework, anyway."

If you want healthy kids after a divorce, they have to understand that the other parent will be consulted if an important decision has to be made. You must appear as a united front even if your ex-spouse drives you crazy, because children will eventually figure out which parent can be manipulated, and then the authority of both parents is undermined. Although you may feel vindicated if you appear to be "the nice one," your children are the ones who suffer.

10. Be Flexible

There will be many times when your original custody agreement will not coincide with special events in your children's lives. For example, in my own case, my ex-husband's parents came to town unexpectedly on my weekend with our daughter. She had not seen her grandparents for quite a while, but she was not scheduled to see her father for another week, and his parents were returning home in a few days. When my ex-husband phoned to see if Annie could visit, I was taken by surprise. My inclination was not to vary the schedule, because I have remarried and now live in a blended family. My husband also has two children from a previous marriage and we try to keep all the kids on the same schedule—everyone home at the same time, everyone at their other parent's home at the same time. However, this was our daughter's first opportunity to see her grandparents in two years, and although it was a little difficult to explain to all the kids why the schedule must change, this was a special occasion.

Decide to deviate from the original custody agreement because of a special event, not because your ex-spouse is seeing your child on "your time." The more flexible you can be, the better adjusted your child will be, which should be your goal.

Counseling: Will It Help My Family?

Everyone is different and whether counseling will help depends on the individual. It is not uncommon for couples to wait too long for counseling. By the time they finally do go for help they are no longer looking to solve problems but want the therapist to referee their arguments. During counseling sessions, the couples keep score, hoping the counselor will announce that they are not the bad person, the reason for the breakup. The counselor hears a lot of "Do you know what *he* did?" or "Do you know what *she* did?" Meanwhile, the children are reeling from the friction in the home, and it may be too late for the therapist to have any impact on the relationship.

"Counseling doesn't work. I went to a counselor with my ex-wife, once. He said he couldn't help us," says Luis Gonzales of

Pleasanton, California, who received counseling through his Kaiser Permanente HMO. But what he failed to mention was that he and his ex-wife had been fighting on and off for five years. By the time they decided to go to counseling, it was their last-ditch effort to make the marriage work. Gonzales had already moved out of the house and was no longer committed to the relationship. He went to counseling to appease his wife, who desperately wanted to reconcile. They had simply waited too long to try to fix their problems. The counselor recognized this in their first session and told them upfront that they had waited too long.

Waiting too long to go to family counseling is easy to do. Time passes quickly. Parents are bogged down by the everyday concerns of putting food on the table and paying the bills. When you walk through the door at the end of the day, you just want the problems to disappear. The fact that your daughter from your first marriage is constantly arguing with your new wife is a problem that will work itself out. Or is it? Sometimes family problems do heal with time, but at other times a good counselor is all that is needed to get a family back on track.

"How long will this all take?"

That depends on you, the weight of your problems, and your commitment to solving them. It is common practice that as you begin counseling you meet with a therapist once a week for about fifty minutes. If you need to see the counselor more or less often, he will advise you. Give him time to build a relationship with you, consider your problem, and work out a strategy that works for you. Just as the problem did not happen overnight but grew to the point where you and/or family members needed help through counseling, so it may be that finding a solution may also take a while. But, beware, if you do not seem to progress to the problem-solving stage within a reasonable amount of time, the coun-selor you have chosen may not be right for you. That's when you should look for another counselor.

"Where do I find a good counselor?"

If you have never been to a therapist before, selecting one may re-quire a little research.

- Start with friends. Ask those who have sought counseling what they thought of their therapist. Would they return to her if they had another problem? If so, she is a good prospect.
- Ask if they have family counselors in your child's school dis-trict. If they do not, they will have names on file that they can suggest.
- Try your church or synagogue. Your priest or rabbi may not only be a source for guidance, but may also be able to recom-mend the name of a trusted counselor.
- HMO facilities usually have staff counselors, and this service is part of your medical plan. Or, ask your family doctor if she can suggest a good family counselor.
- Each state has some sort of facility to help provide mediation and orientation to divorcing parents seeking help with cus-tody disagreements, alimony, and child support. For example, in California, it is called Family Court Services. This service may not be called Family Court Services where you live. Call the family court division of superior court in your county to find the proper agency. Find the phone number in your phone book, or call Directory Assistance.
- Insurance agencies may require you to use a specific coun-selor in order for the sessions to be covered by your medical insurance. Check with your medical health-coverage carrier for suggestions of potential counselors.

A Divorce Casualty—When Counseling Helped

Felice was nine when her parents decided to separate. They knew from the day they separated that they were getting a divorce, but Felice was led to believe that someday her parents might reconcile. Six months later, when her mother received her divorce papers in the mail, Felice opened them by mistake. She could read well enough to know what the papers were, and her sweet personality immediately changed to angry and vindictive. She was not only upset that her parents were getting a divorce, but she also felt betrayed, thinking Mom and Dad had kept something as serious as their divorce from her. It wasn't because, as all parents do, they were trying to protect her, but because in her young mind she feared that she was the cause of their split and they were angry with her.

Counseling helped Felice to realize that her parents' divorce was not her fault. In joint counseling, when Felice's mother also attended, she explained that Felice had been told the divorce was not her fault on many occasions. Felice reasoned, however, that if her parents had lied to her about the divorce, they might have lied to her about the reason for it. She needed to find someone she could trust—in this case, a counselor—until trust was again reestablished with her parents.

Felice's family did get the help it needed through counseling. Each member learned to deal with their own problems, but it took ten months of weekly sessions to break through Felice's anger and frustration.

As a parent, you should know that if your child is manifesting negative behavior as a result of your divorce, it may take months to break through to clarity and understanding. Counseling is not a quick fix. It is a commitment you must make to help find solutions.

"Is there anything positive about this divorce?"

At first glance, probably not. Most divorces are a crisis. Unless the divorce ends some type of emotional or physical abuse, every member of the family is probably upset. After the dust settles, if you look at your divorce objectively, is there anything positive you can teach your children from this experience?

The answer is, of course, yes. You can be solid role models. You can set an example for your children by showing them how to treat someone with whom you obviously disagree, with honesty and respect. If arguments occur, you can show your children how to fight fair—by working for resolution rather than fighting or trying to prove your ex-spouse wrong. You can teach them not to be vindictive but to approach all obstacles by using fair judgment. And you can prove to them you love them above all.

CHAPTER TWO

Where to Begin?

"Problems can not be solved by the same level of think-
ing that created them."

—ALBERT EINSTEIN

I remember overhearing a conversation years ago while at a park with my children. It was between two women, both mothers, who were discussing the recent divorce of a mutual friend. "Who won custody of the children?" asked one of the women.

"Won?" replied the other women, sarcastically. "I'm not sure *won* is the correct word."

Won probably isn't the best word to describe where your child will live after divorce, but it is the word used most often to describe who gets custody. Other commonly used terms are custody *war* or custody *battle*. Divorcing parents don't discuss who should have custody of the children; they *fight* for custody. These phrases depict a warlike dispute, with an armed confrontation being the only answer.

The truth is, there are no victimless divorces. No one wins when a family is severed by divorce, and it is in every family member's best interest that the custody of our children is decided upon by using compassion and love, with as little anger as possible.

First Things First

The first step to deciding the custody of your children is to legally establish who are the parents of the children in question. This may sound easy at first, but in this day and age of divorce, live-in relationships, and single parenting, finding both the birth mother and birth father may be more complicated. To offer a better understanding of the legalities of establishing parenthood, let's look at some of the legal definitions to see what category applies to you.

Biological Parent

The biological parents, birth parents, or natural parents are the people who physically contribute to making the baby: the woman whose egg and the man whose sperm created the child. Generally, these two people are either married or living together, and both have equal rights in seeking custody of their children after separation. However, in the case of artificial insemination or surrogate motherhood, the two biological parents relinquish their rights as parents, and neither may seek custody.

Adoptive Parent

A parent who has legally adopted a child is the adoptive parent. The biological parents have given up all rights and obligations to the child, and the adoptive parents have accepted them. When two adoptive parents separate, both may seek custody.

Psychological Parent

It is rare, but someone may qualify as a psychological parent in the eyes of the court if they are seeking *visitation* with a child after having established an emotional bond that, if terminated, is deemed detrimental to the child. A psychological parent is not financially responsible for the child.

Equitable Parent

In some states, specifically Michigan, Wisconsin, and New Mexico, custody and/or visitation has been granted to someone who is not the biological parent if they are found to be of great emotional or psychological support to the child, for example, a man who has been married to the biological mother and raised her child as his own but is not the child's biological father. The equitable parent theory comes into play when a spouse and child have become close through long association and regard themselves as parent and child. If someone is granted equitable parent status by the court, they may receive custody or visitation but must also accept the responsibility of child support.

Stepparent

A stepparent is someone who is married to the child's biological parent. A stepparent does not automatically have any legal obligation to the child. They are not responsible for support, nor are they automatically granted visitation when they are divorced from a child's biological parent. A stepparent has a few approaches to take to gain legal visitation of their former stepchildren. They can petition the court for psychological parent status, which is a long-drawn-out process, or they can seek visitation as part of their divorce decree from the biological parent. For example, Section 3101(a) of the California Family Legal Code is set aside specifically for stepparents. Summarized, it stipulates that stepparents may petition for visitation. If you are a stepparent looking for legal visitation of your former stepchildren, check for the correct section in your state's family legal code.

Acknowledged Father

When the parents are unmarried, a man is found to be the acknowledged father of a child by either his admission to be the father or by an agreement of the parents. To protect the acknowledged father's rights to visitation, if he is found not to be the biological father, it is best to get a court order recognizing his acknowledged father status. An acknowledged father is responsible for child support.

Presumed Father

A man is understood to be the father of a child if he was married to the mother at the time of the conception and/or birth, or was married to the mother after the birth and agreed to have his name listed on the birth certificate and/or support the child. The label *presumed father* can even be associated with a man who received a child into his home and openly regarded that child as his own but may not be the biological parent.

It can be tricky to be regarded as the presumed father, so know your rights. In some states, if you are regarded as the presumed father it can never be disproven, even if blood tests prove otherwise (Michael H. v. Gerald D., 491 U.S. 110 [1989]).

Unwed Father

When an unmarried man impregnates a woman, he is regarded as an unwed father. Unless the unwed father also accepts his responsibilities as the presumed father, he has little say concerning the welfare of the child. An unwed father may not interfere with the mother's decision on abortion or adoption, and if the mother decides to keep the child after it is born, the unwed father then may be required to support the child. If the unmarried man is acknowledged as the father by the court, he can then seek visitation and custodial rights.

The Second Step

The second step in deciding custody of your children is to understand some of the terminology associated with custody.

"What does custody *mean?"*

Custody, as defined in Webster's Unabridged Dictionary, is "keeping; guardianship; care." If you are granted legal custody of your children, you are legally responsible to house, feed, clothe, and care for them. All decisions regarding where they will live, medical care, religious upbringing, and education are the sole responsibility of the parent who has been awarded legal custody.

"What do custodial *and* noncustodial *mean?"*

The parent who is awarded physical custody, or the right to have their child live with them, is the custodial parent. The noncustodial parent refers to the parent who does not have custody. The noncustodial parent is usually granted visitation and is required to pay child support.

"Please explain the terms sole custody *and* visitation."

If you have sole custody of your children and your ex-spouse has visitation, this means your children live with you, and you alone are the decision maker in regard to their physical and emotional welfare. They visit your ex-spouse on designated days set aside by the court. The frequency of these visits is decided upon at the time of your divorce. You may deviate from the visitation agreement by allowing your ex-spouse to see the children more often than agreed upon in your divorce decree, but it is illegal to deny your ex-spouse his visitation rights. You must follow the letter of the custody agreement. If your custody agreement states that your child should see your ex-spouse every other weekend, for example, your child must be available to your ex-spouse on those proposed days. Legally, it must be the noncustodial parent's decision to not take advantage of their visitation.

The noncustodial parent is usually required to pay child support to the custodial parent. The everyday care of the child is regarded as the custodial parent's contribution to the child's upbringing.

"What's the difference between joint custody, shared custody, physical custody, and joint physical custody?"

The terms *joint custody* and *shared custody* are often interchangeable and refer to the same custody solution. When parents are awarded joint or shared custody, they legally share the responsibilities of raising their children. However, the child does not have to spend an equal amount of time with each parent, and parents do not have to be married or living together to be awarded joint custody

Physical custody refers to *where* the child legally resides. Joint *physical* custody means the parents share in the decision-making process of raising the children, but the children also *physically* reside an equal amount of time with each parent. To clarify, here's an example of each type of joint custody.

Joint custody: Janet and Michael Murphy divorced fifteen years ago, when their daughter, Adrianne, was only nine months old. Adrianne lives with her mother and visits her dad on weekends and alternating holidays. Janet and Michael speak at least twice a week to discuss Adrianne's schooling, religious training, health, etc. All decisions for their daughter's welfare are made together.

Janet has *physical custody* of their daughter, which means Adrianne resides with her mother, but the joint custody option allows Michael to remain active in his daughter's life, help make decisions for her, as well as gives him the right of consent should she want to marry, enlist in the armed services, or become emancipated before the age of eighteen.

Joint physical custody: Beatrice and Will Furgeson have two children. Upon their divorce they were awarded joint custody and joint physical custody. This means the children will reside 50 percent of the year at Mom's and 50 percent of the year at Dad's. The decision was that Gary and Jack, ages six and eight, live the first two weeks of each month with Beatrice and the second two weeks of each month with Will. Beatrice and Will live a mile from each other so that their children can attend the same school and maintain friendships.

What is "bird's nest" custody?

Bird's nest custody is a joint custody agreement that allows the children to remain in the home while the parents move in and out at regular intervals.

"On what do the courts base their decisions when deciding final custody?"

All decisions are based on *the best interest of your child*. But, as with all legal matters, what you believe to be the best interest of your child and what the court believes may be two different things. That is why, if possible, it is best to make custody decisions with your ex-spouse, because unless abuse has been proven on the part of one parent or the other, the courts often grant the wishes of the parents concerned. The court bases its opinion for awarding custody on such concerns as:

- *Who was the primary caregiver before the separation?* The goal here is to not upset the child's normal, everyday activities. Did the mother stay home while the father worked? Did the father stay home while the mother worked? If the mother worked outside the home, how much time did the child spend at day care, and if custody was granted to either party, how would that affect the already-established living pattern?

- *How old is the child?* While mothers are not necessarily awarded primary custody of very small children, the court does take age into consideration. It also considers the wishes of older children. For example, if a twelve-year-old boy wishes to remain with his father after the divorce, the court takes this request very seriously when awarding final custody.

- *Who can supply the best living environment (i.e., type of neighborhood, schools)?* Are there siblings to be considered? Courts do not like to split custody of brothers and sisters unless necessary. If there are other children in the home, most courts will make one decision concerning all of them, but there are always exceptions to the rule. For example, when multiple marriages are involved and perhaps half siblings, who will be affected by a child leaving in a custody dispute, the court looks at the entire picture before granting final custody.

- *The ability for a parent to provide for the child (i.e., salary of each parent).*

- *The mental and physical health of the parents.* Is there any history of drug use or abuse of any sort?

"I don't make as much money as my ex-husband does, but I still want sole custody of my children."

Your personal income is just one consideration in determining who receives custody of the children. To reiterate, decisions are made *in the best interest of the child.* You will hear this phrase often. This means the court weighs all determining factors and then makes the final decision based on what it believes is best for the child.

The fact that someone does not make as much money as their ex-spouse is why child support was established—to supply or supplement the custodial parent's income. A mother who chose not to work outside the home but stayed home to take care of the children obviously cannot contribute the same financial support to her children as the husband who holds a paying full-time job.

If you are found to be the primary caregiver before the divorce, there is a real possibility you will receive primary custody of your children after your divorce, and child support will be ordered paid to the custodial parent by the noncustodial parent.

Now let's look at this another way. Wanting sole custody of your kids does not mean you will receive it. If your ex is also a stable and viable parent and wishes to share custody, the court will most likely decide that this scenario is in the best interest of the child and award joint custody. (Chapter four explains joint custody.)

"What if one parent threatens the other parent during a divorce battle with getting sole custody of their children and then moving away with them after the divorce is final? And, to further add insult to injury, they threaten that if the other parent does receive custody, no child support will be paid."

Unless the court finds parents to be unfit, it is unlikely an ex-spouse will receive sole custody of the children if the other parent wants to continue to be active in the children's lives and *asks for shared custody* in the divorce decree. Of course, there are always extenuating circumstances, but in this day and age, considering typical divorce and custody problems, a parent has a better chance of receiving joint custody than sole custody if both parents are found fit and both want custody of their children. Your divorce decree can stipulate that children not be permanently taken out of the state or even the county.

Addressing the child support issue, it is a federal offense to move to another state to avoid paying child support. (We'll discuss this in chapter eight, "Child Support: Payment, Collection, and Modification.")

"Who has custody of our children until our divorce is final?"

When a divorce is imminent, a couple may go to court to request temporary custody orders until the divorce is final. Don't be misled, however, because these are called *temporary orders*. Although the temporary orders do not always remain in effect after the divorce is final, they are thought to constitute the grounds for your final custody agreement. Judges do not like to disrupt the lives of children any more than they have to. If the temporary custody orders are working, they are likely to stand.

Tiffany Woodruff wanted a divorce from her husband of six years. She longed to return to school to get her degree in interior design. Her verbal agreement with her husband, Tyrone, was that their three children would reside with him until she enrolled in school and secured a new place to live. She would then take custody of Roy, three; Lucy, four; and Michael, five and a half. Temporary orders were issued to Tyrone, and Tiffany began doing exactly what she had proposed. In two months' time she had rented a three-bedroom apartment and enrolled in the nearby state college.

Tiffany and Tyrone had agreed that Tiffany would regain custody *when* she "got organized," but "organized" did not mean the same thing to Tiffany as it did to Tyrone. He would not release the children when Tiffany was ready, and since the temporary orders issued gave Tyrone temporary custody, the children were legally bound to stay with him. Since the children were flourishing and appeared to have no emotional problems because of Tyrone's custody, the court found no reason to alter the temporary custody orders when the divorce became final.

Remember, everything in terms of custody decisions is done in the best interest of the child. If, during the time of temporary custody, a parent exercises bad judgment, interferes with the other parent's visitation, or the child seems to have trouble adjusting, and behavioral or emotional problems develop, all of this is weighed at the time of the final divorce decree, and changes can be made.

"Who gains temporary custody?"

Gayle and Paul Maas decided to divorce four years ago. They had two children, ages twelve and fourteen. Paul was a chiropractor and had converted the in-law quarters above their garage into his office. Gayle was a talk-show host at a local radio station. They both wanted custody of their children.

When Paul and Gayle decided to separate they decided that Gayle would temporarily move in with her parents, while Paul remained in the home with his practice. To prevent further trauma, the children also remained in the home. Gayle then filed a motion with the court, requesting a preliminary hearing on the use of the home and further custody of the children.

It is likely the court will grant Paul temporary custody of the children based on the fact that his practice is in the home and the children are living with him. If Gayle had another lifestyle, say, she worked part time and the children were younger than five, Gayle may have had a better chance for temporary custody. But since she works full time and does not have a place for her children, Paul is the most likely candidate to receive custody. It is also likely that these temporary orders will not change unless Paul and Gayle can come to some other mutual decision.

"What if I do not like the temporary orders?"

If you are not content with your temporary custody agreement, ask for a review by the judge. But have all your ducks in a row. A judge will not make changes based simply on your desire for a change. You will have to prove how a change will be in the best interest of your child, not in *yours*.

"Does the court automatically award custody to the mother when the children are very young?"

No. In the past, most of the country applied the Tender Years Doctrine, which states that children of tender years, or younger than five, must be awarded to the mother if the parents are divorced. More recently, both mother and father are regarded as having equal rights when seeking custody of their children. If both parents are found to be fit, the most common result is to grant them joint custody, and both parents take an active role in the raising of their children after divorce.

"Must I use an attorney when trying to establish custody of my children?"

No. If you and your ex-spouse mutually agree upon where the children will live and how often they will visit each parent and there is no question of suitability, for example, drug addiction or abuse, then there is no need for an attorney—unless, of course, you have other divorce-related issues that are of concern, such as questions about your property settlement. In that case, an attorney would most likely be used and, although custody and property are two separate issues, the same attorney would handle the entire divorce.

Whether you decide to use an attorney to represent your rights in court, it is now recommended that divorcing parents draw up a parenting agreement, sometimes called a Parenting Plan, which answers all the questions concerning the custody of their children after divorce. A Parenting Plan outlines your agreed responsibilities to your children when your divorce is final. It can be as short or as long as you like, but it should be as specific as possible.

"If my spouse and I write a Parenting Plan for our kids, will the court automatically grant exactly what we want?"

While the court can reject any agreement suggested by the parents, the Parenting Plan will most likely stand unless the court finds it is not in the best interest of the child.

Think about it. If you were a judge making decisions for a family you have never met based on paperwork placed in front of you, wouldn't you be able to make a more educated decision for that family if you could refer to something the parents had drawn up, explaining how they plan to raise the children after they divorce? Take the Parenting Plan seriously.

A Parenting Plan may include, but is not limited to:

- Who has legal custody and what type? (Further explanation of the types of available custody will be discussed in future chapters.)
- What decisions are shared? Are all major decisions to be discussed or are decisions made by the parent with whom the children reside, as in the case of joint custody?
- Where the children will live
- Holiday schedules

- How often the children see the other parent, listing visitation schedule
- Transportation to and from each home, including specific drop-off points
- Child support
- Child care
- Insurance for the children (It is not uncommon that a separate life-insurance policy be purchased to ensure that child support continues in case of death of the noncustodial parent.)
- Who is responsible for health care, education, religious training?
- Establish ground rules for changes, protocol. For example, when can a noncustodial parent take a child on vacation? For how long? How far in advance should the other parent be notified?
- How will conflict be handled? Agree upon a specific plan for problem solving.
- Anything pertinent to the family situation

Parenting Plans can be personal. For example, when reviewing one Parenting Plan, I found the mother had listed "Father will make children brush their teeth when they are in his care." This was obviously a past problem about which the mother felt so strongly that she formally listed it in the Parenting Plan attached to their divorce decree.

Another Parenting Plan maintains that when the custodial parent goes out on a date or needs additional child care, the non-custodial parent must be asked to supply child care before a baby-sitter is employed. This solution was suggested by a father who did not receive custody of his children upon his divorce and was bound to a rigid visitation schedule. Looking for an equitable way to see his children more often, he asked that this stipulation be added to his parenting agreement. This was a true custody solution. Allowing the noncustodial father to baby-sit when the custodial mother was out supplied the additional time the father wanted with his children and offered the mother trusted child care.

Jo Boswell of Bend, Oregon, was concerned that her boys were not being fed at their normal dinnertime when they were with their dad. He returned the children to their mother's home at the proper time, 7:00 P.M., but Jo found herself with whining, hungry children on more than one occasion. This was a source of frustration for her and simply reminding her ex-husband that he should feed the kids before he brought them home was not working. She suggested adding to their Parenting Plan that whomever had the children at 6:00 P.M. was to feed them. She felt that if this were formally listed as a requirement in the agreement, her ex would know she meant business. He agreed, and it became a requirement both he and Jo had to meet.

Sound overwhelming? Take one step at a time. The Parenting Plan is supposed to make your life simpler, not frighten you.

"My ex-spouse and I do not feel comfortable writing a Parenting Plan by ourselves."

If you don't feel comfortable writing a Parenting Plan yourselves, there are two approaches you can take: One, you can employ a divorce and family mediator, or you can go to an attorney. In some counties, courts require mediation, and the mediator will even go to court with you should questions arise.

"What is the difference between a mediator and an attorney?"

A mediator is an unbiased third party who is specifically trained in mediation, or, that is, problem solving. They are employed to help you and your ex-spouse reach an agreement together rather than fight it out in court, where the final decision will be taken from you—you are essentially at the mercy of the judge. If you use a mediator to help you write a Parenting Plan, he will listen to the concerns of both you and your ex-spouse and then help you draw up an agreement for the custody of your children based on logic rather than emotion. You and your ex-spouse are asked to sign the agreement as a measure of good faith, and then it can be added to your final divorce decree.

It is important to note that a mediator is not an attorney or an officer of the court and cannot dictate law to you or your ex-spouse. Their goal is to help you and your ex-spouse reach decisions on your own.

Don and Brenda, a divorcing couple from a small town outside Detroit, met twice with the mediator for about three hours each meeting. They took the agreement they designed with the mediator to an attorney to put into legal form, and it was then added to the final divorce decree. "The judge complimented us on our divorce. He was impressed by our commitment to our children and not being petty," Don explains. "We have had problems and we did go back to the mediator one more time. Our personal agreement to each other is to go to a mediator to solve problems. We try to stay away from attorneys. Neither Brenda nor I can afford thousands of dollars an argument. Our mediator kept us on the straight and narrow, never deviating from what was important—our kids."

If you are so at odds with your ex-spouse that you cannot discuss the custody of your children without heated arguments, then you should employ individual attorneys, but remember, a mediator costs a fraction of what an attorney will charge.

"What is the difference between a court-appointed mediator and a private mediator?"

1. cost
2. number of sessions per case
3. topics covered

First, court-appointed mediators are often free of charge. The mediator probably has a contract with the county, and his services are paid for by the court. You pay a private mediator directly for his services. The amount should be agreed upon before mediation begins. It is either a flat fee for a certain amount of sessions, or you may be charged by the hour, depending on the mediator.

Second, the court may limit the number of mediation sessions available to you if you use a court-appointed mediator, say, three or four sessions per case. A court-appointed mediator may also be restricted to discussing an issue of custody, visitation, for example, and would not be allowed to help you solve additional problems. A private mediator is at your disposal should any issue you desire need his mediation skills, and you may return at your leisure if, down the road, additional problems arise.

Emily and John Tracy of Sacramento, California, used the court-appointed mediator to help them establish their visitation schedule and liked the process so much that they hired a private mediator for other problems that arose after their divorce was final.

"We had some issues as the children got older, and our arguing didn't seem to solve the problems, so we used a mediator to draw up an agreement that, after hashing things out with a third party in the room, allowed us to walk away friends," John says.

"A mediator's job," says Steven Rosenberg, an attorney from Mill Valley, California, who has now converted his law practice solely to mediation, "is to make sure the clients have the kind of conversation that enables both of them to come to a resolution without the assessment of fault or blame." Although he is an attorney, Rosenberg says, he wears another hat as a mediator. "When I mediate I do not represent either client. If an attorney is needed, I make it clear to both parties that counsel may be needed *in addition* to my services."

"What can I expect from a mediator?"

You can expect a fair approach to problem solving. When you walk into a mediator's office he will set the ground rules for you. He will explain what is expected of you and frankly tell you that it is his responsibility to keep you pointed toward your problem-solving goal, not to let you deviate into an argument. He will also explain that he expects basic courtesies, no insulting, cutting remarks, and will allow each person the same amount of time to talk and explain their point of view.

When I mediate, if I find someone is particularly long-winded, I have been known to set a ten-minute time limit for venting. And if the venting serves no purpose toward achieving the final goal, it is not permitted—at least, not at that moment. Therapy for specific problems should be set aside for another time. But there is also another way to look at venting to your ex-spouse: Sometimes the only way to get to the root of a problem is to allow the parties to really hear how the other is feeling. Then they can move on to the problem-solving stage. In that case, a mediator will assess the situation and offer his office as a forum to do just that: *Constructively* vent feelings so that the couple can move past their anger and on to positive resolution.

It is understood that all information, for example, bills and pay stubs, are truthful, and everything mentioned in a mediator's office is regarded as confidential. Therefore, the mediator you choose cannot be called into a court of law to testify about what was said during your mediation session.

"Are mediators licensed?"

There is no formal license for mediation, but there is certification. Certification is often part of a teacher, therapist, or attorney's advanced training in their specialty. For example, someone with an education or psychology background may go into family and divorce mediation, whereas, someone with a business background may specialize in mediation between corporations or labor unions, even employment disputes. Some states have specific requirements that mediators must follow, while others have none, so beware. Attorneys are often certified as mediators. However, it would not be a good choice to have your attorney represent you *and* mediate for you.

"How do I find a good mediator?"

There are a few different ways to find a mediator. As mentioned, some counties require mediation as part of the divorce and custody process. If this is the case, court-appointed mediators will be found in the courthouse. If this is not the case, I always start by asking friends for help. They can tell you firsthand if the mediation process helped them solve a divorce or custody dispute. Next, if you are in counseling, your therapist may have the name of a good mediator, or she may even be a mediator herself. Try your local legal aid society, the Internet, or the yellow pages. Look under *Mediation*.

If you are using an attorney to handle your divorce, don't be afraid to ask him for the name of a mediator. George Thomas, a prominent divorce lawyer in the Silicon Valley area of Northern California, often suggests mediators to his clients but had an interesting take on the subject when asked. "Many clients are so angry with their ex-spouses that they want their day in court. They would rather fight in front of a judge than work it out in private. The divorces of my clients who are open to mediation seem to run much smoother."

Lisa Andrejko, an attorney specializing in family law in California's San Joaquin County, previously practiced in Pennsylvania. "San Joaquin County requires mediation as part of the divorce process, and I can tell you that most divorces run much smoother with the help of a mediator. Pennsylvania did not require mediation, and some of the divorces I handled got quite messy."

Try these other sources when searching for a mediator:

- Academy of Family Mediators
  1500 S. Hwy 100, Suite 355
  Golden Valley, MN 55416
  (612) 525-8670

- Family Law Council
  P.O. Box 217
  Fair Lawn, NJ 07410

- Your county court of family law

Local family law courts often have mediators in the courthouse to help you solve problems before you face the judge.

"When is mediation unadvisable?"

If there is any history of violence or domestic abuse, mediation may not be advisable. In the mediation process, you are in someone's office discussing problems and, together with the help of the mediator, you and your ex-spouse are looking for specific answers to specific problems. A history of violence may make it impossible to calmly discuss a problem, and it is unfair to put both yourself and the mediator in a potentially dangerous position.

If you have your heart set on mediation and there is a history of emotional or domestic abuse, search for a mediator who specializes in such cases. They will have ample security to cope if someone has the potential to be violent. However, I have found when there is a history of domestic violence, arbitration may be the answer.

"What is arbitration?"

A simple definition for arbitration is when a judge, or someone with the legal authority to make decisions, hears the case and decides for you.

"What is litigation?"

When you are in litigation you are party to a lawsuit. Someone is suing you or you are suing someone else. When you are divorcing, for example, although at first you may not think of it as such, you are suing your ex-spouse for a divorce. Therefore, you are in divorce litigation.

"What will an attorney do for me that a mediator cannot do?"

As mentioned, a mediator is not an officer of the court and cannot advise you of the law. Mediators are employed as a third party. They are required to remain impartial and help you and your ex-spouse reach an agreement concerning specific issues.

The attorney's responsibility is to advise you of your legal rights and to represent *your* interests in court.

"Who represents the child's rights?"

If the parents have lost sight of the best interest of their child, it is not uncommon for the court to appoint an attorney to represent the child separate from the parents. In this case, an investigation is usually conducted to decide with which parent a child should reside.

When neglect or abuse is suspected and the family comes before juvenile court, rather than appoint an attorney, some states appoint a Court Appointed Special Advocate (CASA), also referred to as a Guardian *ad litem*, to represent the child's interests. These are extreme cases, when the child has become estranged from the parents and there is a question as to which parent would supply the best environment for the child after divorce. A parent, close relative, attorney, retired schoolteacher, and people interested in the welfare of children have become Court Appointed Special Advocates.

Judy Farrell, a retired community health nurse in Portland, Oregon, became a Court Appointed Special Advocate two years ago, and says, "The CASA's bottom line is to confirm that all means have been taken to reunite the child with his family. When that is impossible due to risk or harm, the CASA advocates for the best possible situation. The CASA does not befriend or act as big sister to the children—she acts as investigator, facilitator, advocate—independent of any agency interests."

I came into contact with Farrell when she was working on a case concerning joint custody of a baby whose parents were not communicating well but were still attempting a placement schedule of one week with each parent. Because of confidentiality constraints, Farrell was not permitted to discuss the specifics of the case but admitted she had not had that much experience when parents were at odds while attempting joint physical custody. She was seeking expert opinions on the subject. It was her job to review the case, make sure joint physical custody was in the best interest of the child, and then make her recommendation to the court.

"When my husband and I separated, I did not want to upset my children further by disrupting their home life, so I left them with him. Now that we have filed for a divorce, he claims I abandoned them and tells me I will lose my right to see them. Is that possible?"

It is important to check the laws in your state *before* you make your move to leave. Some states are more lenient than others, and leaving an ex-spouse does not necessarily constitute abandonment. But, add an angry ex-spouse to a strict family court and you may very well lose your children.

Melissa Brooks of Benton County, Mississippi, left her marriage to Sammy Lee James after seven years and two children. At the time, she was having both emotional and financial problems and it was agreed that their children, ages five and seven, would be better off living with their father in the family home. When filing for divorce, a brutal custody struggle ensued, and Melissa was charged with abandonment. The presiding judge felt her failure to see her children on a regular basis, as well as an unstable home life made her an unfit parent. She lost all parental rights to her children, which enabled them to be adopted by her ex-husband's new wife. An appeal, of course, was made, and the Mississippi Supreme Court ruled 6 to 3 that "the state may not bolt the door to equal justice" for the poor. It also found "few decrees are so grave in their consequence as a court order permanently severing the parent-child bond," but it took more than two and a half years to come to that conclusion. In a case like this, it is difficult to pick the winners or the losers.

"I used to have a drug problem, but I have been clean for four years. I have a job and I have never missed a child support payment, but my ex-wife still makes it difficult to see my kids. What would happen if I just picked them up one day and didn't take them back?"

Again, know the law. You are talking about kidnapping. With your background, even though you have had four years of sobriety, if you do something this desperate, you may be facing fines, an inability to be left alone with your children in the future, and jail time.

Many people have felt kidnapping was the only answer to their custody problems, but more often than not, parents kidnap not for the sake of the children but because of anger toward the ex-spouse. Of course, there are those cases when a parent knows their child is being abused but cannot prove it. These cases, however, are rare.

It is a fantasy to believe you will take your kids, move to another country, and live happily ever after. The truth is, if you do kidnap your children, you are condemning them to a life underground. They may have to change their name, perhaps their very identity, in order to function completely within their new life.

The wounds you impose by kidnapping your children will be even deeper than those created by your divorce. If putting your children first in the wake of divorce is what is truly important, deal with your anger. Don't kidnap your children.

"What if I'm not sure I want a divorce? What if I just want to separate for a while and see what happens?"

Again, know the law before you take this kind of action. Don't just leave if you are concerned about your property settlement or the custody of your children. If you have no intention of getting a divorce but just need a break, now is when you and your spouse may want to try counseling or mediation to solve some unanswered problems.

If you are committed to a legal separation, however, you must file with the courts just as you would when you file for divorce. There will be a division of property, alimony will be paid, if necessary, an order for child support will be entered, and visitation will begin, but a legal divorce will not be granted.

Filing for legal separation is actually a dated way to separate from one's spouse. Today, most couples who decide to divorce separate on their own before filing, so filing a legal separation is unnecessary. They just file for divorce and begin the separation process that way. A legal separation is used when a divorce is unacceptable for religious reasons or a dependent spouse needs medical coverage and cannot qualify for it on their own.

CHAPTER THREE

Sole Custody and Visitation

"There are two ways of meeting difficulties, you alter the difficulty or you alter yourself meeting them."
—PHYLLIS BOTTOME

When couples divorced in the past it was readily accepted that the mother received custody of the children and the father received visitation and paid child support. This was based on the fact that the mother was the primary caregiver and the father was the primary breadwinner. Not so today. The roles of mother and father are not so clearly defined. The mother may not be the primary caregiver but the primary breadwinner. However, today, the father may stay home and take care of the kids, which is why mothers are not automatically granted custody of the children, even if the children are very young. A father has equal ability in the eyes of the law to gain custody of the children after divorce.

This chapter will examine sole custody and visitation, with a panel of parents who have chosen this custody solution after they divorced. They come from all walks of life, from all over the country, and from various ethnic groups. You will read firsthand why they made this choice, what the outcome has been, and how their children were affected.

"What can we expect if we choose sole custody/visitation custody solution?"

If you have sole custody of your child, that means you *alone* have complete *control* of your child's upbringing. All decisions concerning his health and welfare are your responsibility. Your child will live with you, and your ex-spouse will have some sort of visitation and probably pay child support. Let's look at the types of available visitation.

Fixed Visitation

If parents are incapable of communicating after divorce, the court usually assigns a fixed visitation schedule. The days, time, and place for pickup and delivery of the children is ordered by the court and becomes part of the divorce decree.

When the mother receives sole custody, this means the children live with her and visit their father. In the past, standard visitation has been every other weekend; however, this can be modified to suit your lifestyle. Take the case of Bill and Marion Simmons of Las Vegas, Nevada, two of the selected parent panel members.

"When we divorced I was very bitter," recalls Marion. "Bill had secretly gambled away all our savings, and when I found out, I was devastated. I demanded custody of our children, ages four and six, and I would not allow Bill any additional time with the kids other than what was set aside in our original divorce decree, which stated that Bill was to see Gretchen and Alexander from 9 A.M. Saturday morning to 7 P.M. Sunday evening, every other weekend. That was it."

Susan and Joseph Diamond of San Jose, California, had a similar agreement, where one parent assumed sole custody of the children. But after much discussion, it was Joseph who received custody of their two boys, Joel, nine, and Joseph Jr., ten, while Susan received visitation and had to pay child support.

When the boys were young Susan accepted most of the parenting responsibilities, but she had returned to law school and was now a deputy district attorney. As the boys grew older, Joseph became more involved, picking them up after school and coaching their Little League games. This gave Susan more time to pursue her career. By the time Joseph and Susan decided to divorce, their parental roles were dramatically reversed.

As a commercial artist, Joseph worked from his home, using an extra bedroom as his office. It was difficult for Susan to accept, but because Joseph lived and worked in the home, the court felt it would be less disruptive for the boys if Joseph were awarded custody. As a result, Susan became bitter, and communication with Joseph was difficult.

To stay organized while working from his home and raising two boys, Joseph requested that the court set up a visitation schedule. Susan would see the boys every other weekend, with an extra weekend thrown in for good measure every other month. Susan would have to request the weekend in advance in order to give Joseph ample time to prepare the boys. In time, Susan's anger toward Joseph lessened, and she had to admit that the fixed visitation schedule suited her well. "My busy work schedule allows me little free time," she says. "Knowing exactly when I am to see my sons lets me plan my schedule months in advance and allows us quality time together."

Reasonable Visitation

The key word in this type of visitation is *reasonable*. This form of visitation takes into consideration that you communicate well with your ex-spouse and can be flexible. Reasonable visitation usually means allowing the parents to design a visitation schedule that works well for them, but one parent still retains sole custody.

Christine and Greg Wong divorced three years ago. Christine received sole custody of their children Billy, twelve; Alicia, ten; and Martin, eight. Greg did not fight for equal custody of his children because he felt Christine would be fair with visitation privileges and "it would just be easier." The parents worked out their own visitation schedule, which was every other weekend and Monday nights for dinner; however, the dinner night was not written in stone.

"Although we have agreed on Monday nights," Christine explains, "sometimes that night is not convenient for either of us, so we switch to Tuesday or Wednesday. It's fine with me, whatever Greg wants to do. As long as he sees the kids. That's the point."

Greg feels as Christine does when it comes to visitation. "My main goal is to stay in my children's lives. I would like to see them as much as I can. Now that Billy is getting older, he likes to spend more time with me, anyway. I'm glad Chris is so accommodating."

When Custody Changes

A common reason custody changes after divorce is because a child grows older and then requests to live with the noncustodial parent. It is not uncommon for a teenage boy who has lived for years with his mother to decide he would now like to live with his father. When this request is made, parents often consent— without dealing with paperwork or court orders. However, at the age of thirteen or fourteen, a child may not legally dictate where he wants to live if the court has already decided upon custody.

Any change in custody must be made in family court. If the divorce takes place when a child is an adolescent and may speak for herself, the court often takes into consideration where she wants to live.

"Do most people go through the hassle of legally changing custody when a child younger than eighteen wants to live with the noncustodial parent, and both parents agree to the change?"

Many divorced parents simply take the responsibility upon themselves and allow a modification of the custodial agreement. This is referred to as a *stipulated modification,* and it is not necessary to obtain a court order. However, there may be repercussions if changes are made without court approval. If, for any reason, one of the parents decides to abandon the new agreement, it would be impossible to prove the change was made, unless approved by a court. Even a simple note explaining the change in the custody agreement will prevent future arguments.

At fifteen, Robert Cardoza began to break the family rules and stay out beyond his curfew. When counseling didn't seem to curb the behavior, Robert's mother decided it was time for her son to move in with his father. Robert was anxious for the switch. He preferred his father's lifestyle and friends, which made the decision an easy one for all concerned. However, no court paperwork was ever modified. The divorce decree granting Robert's mother sole custody stayed the same.

Upon turning sixteen, Robert obtained his driver's license. He was driving his father's car and had an accident. There was an estimate of damage to the other car for $4,500. Although illegal in the state of California, Robert's father had no car insurance and he refused to pay for the damage, saying that although Robert was living with him at the time, his mother was still legally the custodial parent and therefore responsible for the damage. Since no changes were ever made in the custodial agreement, legally she *was* still the custodial parent and a legal battle ensued.

Alice and Desmond McKinley had an amicable divorce and agreed that Alice would have custody of their nine-year-old son, Andrew. But Desmond missed his son terribly and looked for a way to spend additional time with him. Desmond's answer came when he changed his workweek to four ten-hour days rather than five eight-hour days. He now had an extra day for Andrew.

Alice was delighted with the extra day to herself and wholeheartedly consented to Desmond's suggestion of an extra Friday every other week. Life was great for about six months, as the extra Friday worked for all concerned, but when Desmond began dating Vicki, and decided to take her on one of his excursions with Andrew, problems ensued. The thought of Desmond with another woman was new to Alice, who flew into a jealous rage and notified police that Desmond had kidnapped Andrew. Alice then produced divorce documents that specifically stated Andrew should be with her.

Needless to say, Desmond was in trouble. The whole misunderstanding could have been avoided if Alice and Desmond had recorded their mutually agreed upon change in visitation with the court.

A Similar Situation With a Twist

Sally and Dave Cummings of Porterville, California, had two daughters, when they divorced five years ago. Sally received custody of Jenna, eight, and Teresa, five. Dave was granted visitation and paid child support. When Jenna turned fourteen she opted to live with her father. Sally consented and Dave stopped paying child support for the daughter who lived with him. At fifteen, Jenna decided to move back in with her mother. By this time the two parents had become so estranged because their child moved back and forth, Sally threatened to sue Dave for the back child support she had not received, even if Jenna was not living with her. On paper, she was always the custodial parent.

The message in both the cases of Robert Cardoza and Sally and Dave Cummings is: If you plan to deviate from your original custody agreement, put the changes in writing. Better yet, have them authorized by family court so you have proof the changes were indeed made.

The Cummings Solution

There is an epilogue to the Cummings' story that was brought to light after the family finally sought counseling, even though Sally and Dave had been divorced for more than eight years. Jenna was an extremely bright but manipulative child. As she grew older she sensed her parents' guilt over not being able to make their marriage work and deduced that she would benefit personally if she kept her parents at odds. Rather than being sensitive to her parents' insecurity, Jenna used it to get special treats: more clothes and a little extra spending money. This kept her family in constant turmoil, but Jenna looked at the situation as if she were the winner.

Divorce affects each one of our children differently. In the Cummings' family, Jenna reacted selfishly, while her younger sister, Teresa, harbored a secret wish that her parents would someday reconcile. But Jenna's selfish behavior did not happen overnight. It evolved over years as the result of the comments and actions of her guilt-ridden parents. Family counseling broke the patterns of bad behavior and taught each member of the Cummings family how to cope with the problems that plagued them. When everyone sat in the same room and began to compare notes, Jenna could no longer use one parent against the other.

Through counseling, Sally and Dave realized the mistakes they had made during the years after their divorce. They began to support one another, and when the children were with them individually, they did not find fault or blame the other parent for making bad decisions. They did not reconcile their marriage, but that was never their intention. Counseling helped the Cummings reestablish a mutual goal: to raise healthy children even though they did not choose to live together. Sally retained custody, with a liberal visitation schedule for Dave.

Supervised Visitation

If the noncustodial parent has a history of sexual abuse, drug use, violent behavior, or any reason that has been found to be a destructive influence on a child, the court will require another adult other than the custodial parent to be present during visitation. The supervising adult must be approved by the court.

In the case of Rick and Angela Hernandez, this was a long-drawn-out process. Rick and Angela were divorced while Rick was in prison. They had three little girls, ages five, three, and two. Both Rick and Angela had drug and alcohol problems, and Angela had been tried but never convicted of prostitution, so temporary custody was assigned to Rick's mother. Angela was allowed supervised visitation of one hour per week. Rick's mother was the supervising adult assigned by the court. As time passed, Angela did nothing to curb her drug use, and her supervised visitation time was decreased even further, to a half hour every week.

Rick had two and a half years of prison life that helped turn him around. He joined Alcoholics Anonymous and went back to school to become a computer programmer. He so improved his life that a year after his release from prison he was awarded custody of his daughters. He is remarried and his daughters are flourishing. Angela is nowhere to be seen, but if she does choose to reenter her children's lives, supervised visitation will again be a necessity until she can prove that she is a fit parent.

"How does one prove they are a fit parent?"

The only time you would have to "prove" you are a fit parent is if you have had problems with drugs, mental illness, or participated in some other activity that could be construed by the court to be unfit. As in the case of Rick and Angela Hernandez, both parents had a history of drug abuse and both were deemed temporarily unfit by the court. This is why Rick's mother became the legal guardian. Until Rick could prove he was clean from drugs and alcohol, reeducated himself so he could support his children alone, and reestablish himself in the community, the court would not allow him to be responsible for his children. Upon his release from prison, Rick was required to see a family counselor and was tested weekly for drugs. His children were also required to see a counselor in order to ascertain how much psychological damage, if any, they had suffered. Before Rick could receive final custody of his daughters, he was required to have a custody evaluation.

"What is a custody evaluation?"

The American Psychological Association, located in Washington D.C., has established guidelines for custody evaluations. They are usually performed by a counseling professional—a family therapist or a psychologist.

Although a custody evaluation is often ordered when there is a possibility that a parent or guardian is mentally ill, the goal of these evaluations is to discern the parent's ability to take care of their children through the trials and stresses of everyday life. It is not to decide upon the parent's mental status. If the court orders a custody evaluation, this does not mean the court sees you as an unfit parent. It means it is trying to decide proper custody placement that is in the best interest of your child.

A custody evaluation involves questions, interviews, and observation. Depending on the circumstances, the evaluation may be done in the therapist's office, at your home, in a park, or anywhere a counselor can successfully observe you interact with your child. Know that the person conducting the evaluation will have all your records and medical charts. If you have a prison record, as Rick Hernandez did, the evaluator will know the circumstances. In his case, when Rick was an addict, his judgment was severely impaired. His last conviction was for assault while under the influence. If you have an addiction, the evaluator will know, so trying to hide well-publicized shortcomings will do no good. The best thing you can do in situations such as these is to be honest. Discuss with candor the steps you are taking toward recovery and your desire to now be a good role model for your children. If you are sincere, the evaluator will see that in your demeanor. In Rick Hernandez's case, the evaluator noted his new dedication to a clean life, and watched Angela's deterioration. Rick received custody. It has been five years without a major setback for Rick and his family. It appears the evaluator made the right choice.

Custody and Abuse

If an allegation of abuse is made, the custody evaluator must determine if it indeed occurred. The child's behavior along with the behavior of the accused parent will be examined. The other parent's behavior will also be evaluated. The evaluator will then try to determine if the accused parent is a danger to the child. This will then be reported to the court, and custody will be determined.

Following is a case when an accusation of abuse was made, which further estranged the child concerned. Make sure, if you do suspect abuse, that it is real and the complaint is not filed for other reasons than the best interest of the child.

Gina McLaughlin was not married but had been living with Sean for three years. Gina had a daughter, Connie, from a previous marriage. Sean had a son, and now Gina and Sean had a year-old son together. Gina's ex-husband, Kees, had little to do with Connie over the years. After their divorce, he had returned to his native Holland. Connie was now ten years old and fully assimilated into her new, blended family.

When Kees returned to this country and remarried a woman who could not have children, everything changed. Kees reappeared in Connie's life with promises of trips to Disneyland, her own horse, and a new mother. Connie was petrified. She was afraid her father would take her away from her family.

Kees's new desire to see Connie on a regular basis was met with resistance from all concerned, but Gina recognized Kees's right to see his daughter and consented to a visitation schedule of every other weekend. The schedule was abused from the beginning, with Kees often returning Connie home hours late. A year and a half had passed, when Connie came home with stories of being forced to shower with her father, and Gina was frightened. The truth was, Kees had been brought up in Holland, where nudity is not considered taboo. He thought nothing of showering with his daughter, but this was not done at Gina and Sean's house. The prospect of showering with her father made Connie uncomfortable, and she did not want to return to her father's house. Angry, Kees called Child Protective Services and claimed

Connie was being abused. Since Sean was a hunter, Kees charged, his daughter was being subjected to harmful weapons and perhaps drugs. It was a Sunday afternoon when the police showed up at Gina and Sean's to search the house. They were outside in the backyard barbecuing. They were handcuffed in front of their children for two hours while the police searched their home. They found four hunting rifles, two that were stored in an attic, two in the master bedroom closet. All ammunition was stored in the attic.

As a result of the report, a social worker was assigned to the case and a custody battle began. By this time Connie had turned twelve, and the social worker suggested that a separate attorney be assigned to represent her interests, and custody evaluations were performed on all adults concerned, and Connie was questioned. The case never went to court. Connie, so traumatized by the police search and her knowledge that her father caused it, opted to stop all visitation. She is now fifteen and rarely sees Kees.

What Does This Story Tell Us?

In the United States the word *abuse* sends up red flags, and many agencies become involved. In the Connie McLaughlin case, Child Protective Services, the police department, Social Services, and a court-appointed attorney were all employed because of an allegation of abuse. These are necessary agencies that investigate and protect children from harm. They are not to be used as ammunition to fight a personal vendetta. As a result of Kees's anger, he lost his daughter. He could have handled the situation by discussing the issue with Gina or, if that didn't work, employing a mediator. Together, Kees, Gina, and a mediator could have possibly worked out a more child-friendly visitation schedule, and he would today be enjoying his daughter's company.

Custody and Stepparents

Glen and Barbara Jean Watson are in the process of getting a divorce after ten years of marriage. Glen has two children from a previous marriage that Barbara Jean has grown to love over the years. Her greatest fear is that she will not be permitted to see her stepchildren after the divorce is final.

"I have no problem with BJ seeing the kids after we are divorced. I know she loves them and they love her," says Glen. "My daughter, Celia, is sixteen and has built quite a rapport with BJ. Because BJ and I couldn't make it work, I see no reason to make the kids' lives miserable."

But Glen's ex-wife, Melissa, does not share Glen's feelings. Although she and Barbara Jean were amiable during the marriage, Melissa turned cold and uncommunicative during the divorce. Despite Glen's decision, Melissa in no way wanted Barbara Jean to continue to stay in contact with her children.

"Melissa was fighting old-fashion jealousy," explains Tae-Hyun Moon, Ph.D., a psychologist who often works with disputes of this sort. "Melissa's main concern was that the children had built such a strong bond with Barbara Jean and that she (Melissa) no longer had a place in their lives. But," continues Dr. Moon, "after a few counseling sessions, Melissa understood it was in the children's best interest for them to continue their relationship with Barbara Jean who had always been a positive influence on the children. Plus, from my conversations with the children, I assessed the loss of this interaction brought on by Melissa's obvious insecurity could be damaging to the relationship between Melissa and her own children. My assessment was that the children could possibly resent their mother denying them access to a trusted friend in the midst of the uncertainties of divorce." Without knowing it, Melissa was asking her children to choose sides, and since the kids were older, sixteen and seventeen, they voiced their opinion in no uncertain terms to Barbara Jean, but not to Melissa.

"When I realized why Melissa was fighting my visitation," said Barbara Jean, "I just called her and talked to her about it. I had known this woman for ten years. If I couldn't talk to her now, I knew I would have no chance of gaining visitation in the future. I sensed the bottom line was she was afraid the kids liked me best, which was ridiculous. I was never in competition with her for their affection and I came out and told her so." After that heart-to-heart discussion, Barbara Jean sought formal visitation with her stepchildren as part of her divorce decree, and Melissa did not fight her on it.

Diane Samuels was not as lucky. Her husband's ex-wife, Tammy, opposed any sort of visitation with the children. When Diane asked for visitation as part of the divorce decree, Tammy became a party in the case. This allowed Tammy to present evidence against Diane gaining formal visitation of the kids after the divorce. "If I hadn't become a party in the case," explained Tammy, "I would have had no say about who was visiting my children. Diane would have been part of my life forever, and I wasn't interested in sharing my children with someone who had been married to my ex-husband for only two years. My kids are only four and five years old. I am hoping that as they grow they will forget the entire unfortunate mess."

Child psychologists don't necessarily agree with Tammy. Although children often do not remember things as they grow older, trauma is almost always retained as a childhood memory. "How you handle a case like this is critical," Dr. Tae-Hyun Moon reminds us. "With something as crucial to a child's adjustment after divorce as denying them access to a stepparent, I would consult the help of a therapist that is familiar with your case. Hoping your children will not remember trauma does not ensure they will not retain memories of a stressful divorce. My suggestion would be to follow the children's lead. If they express an interest in seeing a former stepparent after divorce, perhaps that is the best course." Dr. Moon also suggests keeping the lines of communication open. "Don't make your child feel guilty if they want to continue a positive relationship with a former stepparent. Understand your child is probably not picking the former stepparent over you. They may simply be striving to keep the amount of change after your divorce to a minimum."

Divorce attorneys questioned on the subject of former stepparent interaction with children of divorce report that Tammy's decision to sever all ties with a former stepparent is not unusual. "It's not uncommon for ex-wives and current wives to become friends," reports divorce attorney George Thomas, "but if it happens it is after a long association. Over time a mother can see that the new stepmother's concern for her children is sincere, and a respectful bond may be formed. If very little time elapses, the standard feelings of resentment and jealousy are still at the forefront. This makes for a messy second divorce. But if enough time has passed and the mother and stepmother have formed a mutual respect for each other, then if another divorce is inevitable, the mother does not view the stepparent as an enemy and some sort of visitation will most likely be possible."

"I have sole custody of my son. My ex-husband has visitation and pays me child support. I would like my son to go to parochial school, but my ex-husband was raised Jewish and so prefers him to go to public school."

Sole custody grants you the final word in all decisions for your children. This knowledge will not prevent arguments when you and your ex disagree, but it is a fact.

"My ex-wife and I have two children. We cannot decide with whom our children will live when our divorce is final. She has proposed that each of us have sole custody of one child."

As a rule, both professionals and family court judges agree it is not a good idea to separate children after divorce. Splitting up the kids is usually a parent's attempt at being fair by allowing each parent to have a child, but studies show that children may not perceive the split that way.

First, the divorce itself interrupts the children's family life. Splitting them up, allowing one or more to go with one parent and the others to go with another just compounds the problem. "I would hate it if my brother didn't go with me to see Dad this weekend," says Brittany Jones, a happy-go-lucky fifth grader whose parents recently divorced. "I don't really like leaving Mom for a few days, so I like it when Stevie's with me. I just feel better. Oh, don't get me wrong. I love Dad," she adds. "That's not what I'm saying. I'm just glad Stevie's always with me."

In her own words, Brittany is explaining that her brother, Stevie, is her only constant in the throes of divorce. Intellectually, she understands that her parents are divorced and she cannot be with them all the time, but her brother offers the comfort of consistency, and she does not like to be without him.

Second, although sibling rivalry is most often regarded as a family problem, it also serves an important purpose. Sandra Wilhoit, a licensed family counselor from Stockton, California, tells us that sibling rivalry can offer positive learning lessons for our children. "Sibling rivalry also teaches brothers and sisters how to share and how to successfully resolve conflict—important lessons for everyday life. And it is important to note that if a child is taken away from a beloved sibling during a divorce, essentially they are getting two divorces, one from a parent with which they no longer live, and one from the sibling they love and may regard as a stabilizing force when things are so uncertain with their parents. Splitting custody of siblings could compound the emotional damage done by the divorce."

Third, a child may misunderstand why the decision has been made for him to live with a particular parent while his brother or sister lives with the other. When ten-year-old Nicholas MacDonald was asked why his older brother lived with their father while he lived with their mother after the divorce, he responded: "Dad loves Josh more. I had to stay with Mom."

Obviously, Nicholas's father did not love one son more than the other, but because the decision was not explained properly to Nick, he viewed remaining with his mother as a punishment. This decision was made in this family because Josh was thirteen years old and experiencing all the normal hormonal changes boys go through at this age. His mother thought Josh would be more comfortable with his father at this time in his life, so her motive was unselfish in origin; but Nicholas's perception was that there must be something wrong with *him* because his father didn't want him. Mom, who didn't want to *lose* both boys in the divorce, kept Nicholas with her. But was this the right answer? Of course, the true reason behind the decision to split custody must be explained to Nicholas in order for him to not feel punished, but during my interviews, Nicholas's mother expressed a fear that if this was made clear to Nicholas, he may also choose to live with his dad, leaving her alone.

Boys With Dad, Girls With Mom?

Current studies report that boys do well when their fathers have sole custody, and girls do well when their mothers have sole custody. In his book, *The Custody Revolution*, Richard A. Warshak, Ph.D., writes, "It has been found that father-custody boys and mother-custody girls were better adjusted than children in the custody of an opposite-sex parent." That is a huge statement, and society may not be ready to grasp everything this implies.

It's logical to believe that when the hormones kick in, the child would much rather discuss these new feelings with a same-sex parent. However, your child's gender is just one factor to be considered when you are trying to decide fair custody. You must also consider your child's self-esteem. How is she adjusting to divorce? Does he need additional nurturing in order to adjust well? What is his current relationship with his father or mother?

We must also consider the social stigma associated with giving up custody of your children—especially for a mother. How often, when asked why her son lives with his father after divorce, do you hear a mother say, "I honestly thought he would be more comfortable with his dad"? If this is said, the listener's response is usually not, "Oh, how unselfish of you," it's, "When did you get out of rehab?"

If custody decisions are truly to be made in the best interest of the child, then each decision must be made on an individual basis, using love, not ego or fear of loneliness, as the primary factor.

"My ex-husband has legal custody of our thirteen-year-old son. As the noncustodial parent, may I take him out of state to visit his grandparents this Christmas?"

It is best to get written permission from the custodial parent. That way, if something unexpected happens, you have proof you are within the law to take him out of state.

"As the noncustodial parent, may I sign legal documents for my child?"

If your ex-spouse has sole custody of your child/children, he/she is the legal guardian and is the one who signs all legal documents.

"My ex has sole custody of our son but does not make it easy for me to see him. What can I do?"

Studies show that when one parent makes it difficult for the other parent to see their child after divorce, visitation may become sporadic or possibly stop altogether. Although this may have been the eventual goal of the parent causing the trouble, it is not in the best interest of their children. It may also directly impact the consistency of child support payments. Someone who is not permitted to see their children is less likely to send those checks on a regular basis.

There are times when the ex-spouse does not want to participate in the upbringing of their children after divorce. We have all heard the horror stories of deadbeat dads or moms and the psychological and emotional impact their lack of interaction inflicts upon their children after divorce. In these cases, the custodial parent has no choice but to fend for themselves, and the child must survive with only one caring parent. But if you have a loving, supportive parent who wants to participate in their child's life and you sincerely desire a well-rounded, emotionally stable child after divorce, although it may not be something you want to face, interaction with both parents is the best thing for your child.

Louis Espinoza of Los Angeles was eleven when his father, Abel, and his mother, Lisa, divorced. Abel had a problem with fidelity during their marriage, which greatly angered Lisa, so after the divorce was final, she simply went shopping with Louis on Abel's designated visitation days. When Abel questioned her, she told him that they went shopping because Louis needed shoes or a new shirt, or that Saturday was the day for Little League tryouts, and she conveniently forgot to tell him about it. Abel would try to pick up Louis, but his son was never at home.

Lisa was angry because of the years of infidelity. Her goal was to punish Abel, and her only ammunition was their child. Secretly, she felt if she kept Louis from his father, Abel would suffer as much as she had over the years. But, of course, this plan back-fired. Without the care and interaction of his father, Louis felt as if his life were coming apart. He had no direction and no center, and when a local gang member approached him with the family philosophy of gang membership, Louis was immediately attracted.

When Louis began participating in criminal activity at thirteen, Lisa realized the error of her ways. Who had her anger really hurt? The answer was obvious.

If you are faced with custody or visitation interference, your first step should be counseling and mediation. If your ex-spouse will not cooperate with you either by refusing to attend counseling or not showing up for mediation, then you should file a motion with the court to evaluate your custody agreement. In some states, interference in visitation or custody agreements is a felony and the penalty for the crime is more severe if the child is taken out of state. Some states understand when there is an interference in custody or visitation if the parent fears for either their own or their child's safety. This is a difficult subject to defend on your own. You need legal help.

"What are some ways to increase my time with and ability to stay close to my children even though my ex-spouse has sole custody?"

Be creative! As mentioned, asking to baby-sit while your ex-spouse is out is an excellent way to increase time with your child. Here are other ways to stay close to your children, even if you don't have custody:

- Live close to your children so you can attend their sports events or school plays.
- Become your child's den mother or Girl Scout leader. Sign up to coach Little League.

- If you have time during the day, volunteer in the classroom, or carpool to a special event. Be a chaperone for a school-sponsored field trip.
- Kids love to get mail whether it is from across the country or the next city. Send cards and letters regularly, even if it's just a handwritten "I love you!" Mail it! Then call to make sure they received it.

All of the above are different ways to see your child even if they do not sleep under your roof.

"I don't believe my ex has our children's best interests at heart. How do I modify our original visitation schedule?"

You could hire an attorney, who would fill out all the necessary paperwork and represent you in court. If you cannot afford an attorney, contact the family court in your county. Family court services will supply you with all the needed forms or at least point you in the right direction so you can start the procedure yourself.

Sole Custody and Visitation Parent Panel

"Would you choose sole custody with visitation again?"

When asked about the sole custody/visitation scenario they had chosen, most parents interviewed felt at the time it was the best choice for their children, but some expressed reservations and saw the need for adjustments as time passed.

MARION AND BILL SIMMONS: "As we lived apart," confesses Marion Simmons, "I realized how the limited amount of time with their father really affected the children. Bill traveled for business, and at times he was not in town on his visitation weekend. At one point, the children hadn't seen their father for almost two months. I needed a break and their father missed them terribly. We knew we had to make adjustments, but I absolutely did not want to go back to court. I was afraid once I got in there Bill would sue me for custody and I would lose control of my children."

Many parents are afraid to lose control of their children. Ironically, Bill Simmons expressed the same fear this way. "Do you have any idea how demeaning it is to have to ask permission to see your own kids? I hated it. Ever since Marion and I were married, I had worked hard to support my family. Now I had to ask to see my own kids. I had no say, no control at all."

Living divorced can make both partners feel as if things are out of control. As they jockey for position, the children become their pawns. "When Bill gambled away our life savings," explains Marion, "I felt as if my life was out of control. I needed stability and so did the children. To compensate I became inflexible with Bill's visitation time with the kids. I wouldn't give an inch. I was so angry."

As Marion's anger began to dissipate she became more flexible with the children's visitation schedule. She came to this conclusion not because she wished to grant special privileges to her ex-husband but for the sake of her children. "Our solution was simple. If Bill asked for more time, specifically, if he planned a special outing with the kids, I let him take them. It was just very obvious to me that we needed a less rigid schedule in order for my children to be happy."

To calm Marion's fears, I should point out, it is unlikely the court will alter your custody agreement purely on the whim of the other parent, who now wants custody. If you have been suspected of being an unfit parent because of abuse in the home or drug use, then the court may see a reason to change your original custody agreement. Bill's gambling problem could be a good reason for the court *not* to alter the status of the original custody arrangement. The important thing to remember is that your ex-spouse must petition for the change. It is not an arbitrary decision that happens one day while you are away on vacation.

SUSAN DIAMOND: Even though Susan Diamond was the non-custodial parent, she, too, explained that she would again opt for the sole custody solution. "I have to admit that at times it gets embarrassing. I am a woman, an attorney, and my ex-husband has custody of the kids. When people find that out, they immediately think I either have a mental disorder, drug problem, or I'm a terrible attorney. I am often asked, 'How can an attorney lose her kids?' The truth is, I didn't *lose* them. They just live with their dad. I was very angry when Joel was awarded custody of the boys. I felt like a failure as a mother and I decided to got into counseling. The counselor put me in touch with other women who also did not have custody of their children and I began to see it wasn't a flaw in me, as it was not a flaw in the other women I met. With my hectic schedule the boys would fare far better with their father. It was the least disruptive solution, and if I really love my boys . . . I have to admit, they should live with their dad."

LISA ESPINOZA: When Lisa Espinoza was questioned about the sole custody solution, she also believed it was correct for her family at the time of her divorce. "But, I feel badly that I let my anger for Abel interfere in my judgment when it came to visitation," she admits. "I made Abel's life misearble!" Verbal aggression usually fails to further communication because when you yell at someone, they are inclined to yell back, and you are now in an adversarial relationship rather than looking for a solution. "He needed his father in his life," continues Espinoza. "But I couldn't see that in the beginning. I was too angry."

DAVE CUMMINGS: Dave Cummings tells us he would have gone to counseling sooner. "I figured I was divorced. What's counseling going to do for me? But I was wrong. I was so angry with Sally, I couldn't see the forest for the trees. It didn't matter if we were married or not. And to think Jenna just made things worse. When I realized that, I had to admit how detrimental this divorce had been on my children. That was a real wake-up call, and I had to do everything I could to improve things. I approached counseling with an open mind and it really helped. Sally could see I was really trying and that made her want to try, too. Now our visitation schedule is less structured, and since Sally and I talk more, Jenna is less able to manipulate the situation. Things are much better for everyone."

Don't Let Anger Be Your Guide

Suppressed hostility can estrange you from those you love, as in Susan Diamond's case. In truth, Susan's anger had more to do with how she felt about herself than how she felt about her divorce. In her own words, she "felt like a failure as a mother," and her sons knew something was wrong. They, as children often do, thought they were the reason for their mother's anger and, not understanding what they had done, were uncomforatble when they were with her.

SUSAN DIAMOND: "I was not only separated from my husband, my anger was separating me from the children I loved. I had to let my old anger go and look toward the future. My goal became to build a relationship with my sons different from when we all lived together, but solid and one on which they could depend."

CHAPTER FOUR

Joint Custody

"Life affords no higher pleasure than that of surmounting difficulties, passing from one step of success to another, forming new wishes and seeing them gratified."
—SAMUEL JOHNSON

When you choose joint custody of your children as your custody solution, you agree to discuss with your ex-spouse all decisions about your child's welfare. However, parents may initially find the concept of joint custody perplexing, because they confuse the custody of their children with *where* their children live. Where your children live after divorce is referred to as *child placement*, and choosing joint custody does not guarantee that your children will spend equal amounts of time with you and your ex-spouse. When a child spends 50 percent of her time with each parent, that is *joint physical custody* (we will explain that custody solution in the next chapter). Joint custody, simply stated, means *both* parents have equal decision-making rights and responsibilities concerning their children, and agree to discuss important issues before final decisions are made. Both parents may also sign their children's legal documents. (The placement of your child is a separate issue and will be discussed later in this chapter.)

"What is the difference between sole custody and joint custody?"

The main difference between *sole custody* and *joint custody* is the approach. When choosing sole custody, you are accepting full responsibility for your child. No one will help you in the decision-making process. If you choose joint custody, you are agreeing to consult your ex-spouse on all decisions. Issues such as your child's education, religious upbringing, medical treatment, marriage before age eighteen, early enlistment in the armed forces, emancipation, and consistency in discipline are discussed on a regular basis. Joint custody means you have a person who loves your children to talk to when making decisions. Sole custody puts the burden of all decisions on your shoulders alone.

Truth be told, there are times when joint custody does not seem that much different from sole custody. For example, if the children live with one parent and visit the other, and child support is paid to the parent with whom the children live, this sounds like sole custody. But you can also share custody of your children with your ex-spouse, with your ex-spouse having sole *physical custody* of the kids. Translated from legalese, this means you make all decisions together, child support is paid but the kids still live with your ex-spouse, and a liberal visitation schedule is designed to meet the needs of all concerned.

"Will joint custody harm my children?"

First of all, divorce is harmful to your children, so no matter how you look at it, your children will be affected. Second, professionals disagree on whether joint custody is detrimental to a child. Just as many say it is as it isn't. A positive vote for joint custody was found in a recent study out of Denver, Colorado, conducted at the Center of Policy Research by Dr. Jessica Pearson and Dr.

Nancy Thoennes. Over nine hundred parents who chose different types of child custody were interviewed. Parents with joint custody of their children after divorce were found to be more willing to cooperate with the other parent and learned to problem solve more effectively. The study also found divorced parents with joint custody to be less critical of their ex's parenting skills.

No one can predict if joint custody will be detrimental to your children. You are the best judge of that.

"If we choose joint custody, how often may I see my child?"

The percentage of time the child lives with each parent is mutually agreed upon by the parents before the divorce is final. It could be the conventional option, where the child lives with mother, and father has visitation. It could be 80/20, even 70/30, but it must be mutually agreed upon by the parents and then designated in the divorce decree.

If you cannot make this decision together easily, enlist the help of a mediator, whose job it is to help you come to a conclusion. But these are the types of discussions you will have on a regular basis if you choose joint custody. If you are having trouble coming to a conclusion regarding the placement of your child, you may have the same problem with other topics, so joint custody may not be the solution for you.

Practical Placement

David and Beth Wilkinson chose joint custody for their children, Lisa, three, and David, four, when they divorced after five years of marriage. The placement ratio they agreed upon was 70/30, which meant the children would reside with Beth 70 percent of the time and David 30 percent. This worked out fine when the children were young, because David lived in the same town and the same school district, and their placement schedule was flexible. But three years later, David's employer transferred him from California to Kentucky. He did not want to lose time with his children and would not agree to alter the original custody agreement.

To keep the placement ratio as it was, the children were required to reside with David 110 days out of the year. Much to Beth's dismay, it was decided the children would spend the summers with their father. This seemed the most equitable exchange, because although the children did not spend the entire 110 days with David, there was no school in the summer and the children could travel. "At first, I absolutely hated the compromise. The children were gone for such a long stretch of time, and I missed them terribly," she says. "But then I realized how their father must feel the rest of the year, and I had to consent."

David and Beth went one step further. "I know you are going to think we are crazy, but this was our solution. David's job paid very well. After two years of attempting this new custody arrangement, David suggested I move to Kentucky. He was paying me alimony and child support. The cost of living was far more expensive in California than in Kentucky. He said he would help with the move. Plus, if we lived in the same town, our visitation schedule could go back to the way it was. I wouldn't have to go for three months without seeing the kids.

"My first response was 'No way. Why should I change my entire life because my ex-husband was transferred.' But then I thought about it. What was keeping me here? Next month, I'm moving to Kentucky. David is really trying to help me get organized. I mentioned I wanted to get a part-time job, and he arranged an interview with a sister company. The kids are old enough. It's time for me to go back to work."

Perhaps David and Beth's solution—an ex-wife moving closer to the ex-husband so they can raise their children together—seems atypical. But Beth says, "When we accepted joint custody as a custody solution, we agreed we would raise the children together. This meant we may have to make personal choices we didn't like for the sake of the kids. Our goal was always to put the children first. They did not ask for this divorce, so I felt it was my obligation to make it as easy as possible on them. Moving seemed to be the logical answer."

When Joint Custody Can Help

Elizabeth Davenport of Cincinnati, Ohio, had a traumatic divorce and custody battle. She was a working mother with a career that required her to travel. Without knowing it, her daughters, ages twelve and thirteen, resented the time she traveled for work. They were angry and frustrated, and when their parents decided to divorce, this was just icing on the cake. Her daughters opted to stay with their father.

Elizabeth felt as if she had lost her daughters, and to make matters worse, her ex-husband was suing for sole custody. Elizabeth felt wounded and inadequate as a mother. And since she made almost three times as much money as her ex-husband, she was ordered to pay hefty child support payments. She described the entire episode as "the worst nightmare. I kept thinking the problem would be gone when I woke up."

During mediation, which was required by the court, Elizabeth's husband, Carl, became less angry about the split just long enough to realize how important it was to both the girls and Elizabeth to remain part of her daughters' lives. Joint custody was the answer. The girls would stay with their father, and a visitation schedule was drawn to accommodate Elizabeth's traveling, but the joint custody solution demanded that Carl consult Elizabeth on all decisions concerning the children. Joint custody eased Elizabeth's feelings of inadequacy and made her feel like she was still part of her daughters' lives. She was not just simply a paycheck. She mattered. Joint custody also allowed the girls to stay with their father while dealing with their anger for their mother. Through this process, Elizabeth had a strong presence, even though the girls did not physically live with her.

Carl and Elizabeth's family obviously had issues that were exacerbated by their divorce. Counseling was prescribed for each member of the family, and mediation was suggested for Carl and Elizabeth. Through the counseling and mediation, it was agreed that joint custody was the correct solution, and although the children still live primarily with their father, the arrangement was chosen because it accommodates Elizabeth's traveling schedule, not because of the girls' anger and frustration. The time Elizabeth now spends with her daughters is comfortable and rewarding, and joint custody allows her to be active in her children's lives, even though she does not see them every day.

Another Joint Custody Success Story

Belinda and Michael Mathison divorced fifteen years ago. Their daughter, Susan, was just nine months old at the time. Belinda felt guilty because she initiated the divorce, devastating Michael, who had no idea it was coming. Because of her guilt, Belinda agreed to a joint custody solution, feeling it would appease Michael in some way, but she demanded that Susan live with her. In other words, Belinda and Michael had joint custody of their daughter, but Belinda had sole physical custody and Michael paid child support. This is a perfect example of when sole custody and joint custody are very much the same. It is merely the approach that makes them different.

"At first, Susan was so young I was afraid to leave her with Mike, but in my heart I knew he was a very good father, and I consented to the joint custody. Now that Sue is fifteen and a handful, I am elated that I opted for the joint custody solution. Even though Sue has always lived with me, she regularly visited her dad. He has never missed a child support payment and has always been supportive whenever I called upon him to help with Sue. It is especially helpful to have his ear now, when Sue is so difficult. Fifteen years old hit her hard and I am dealing with all the anticipated behavioral problems—times ten! Since Michael isn't around all the time, he is far less emotional than I am and can bring a logical head to the table. It really helps!"

"If you choose joint custody, how does the court determine who gets physical custody of a child?"

First, it may be easier to refer to *where* your children live as placement rather than custody, because in joint custody both parents have equal legal custody but not necessarily equal placement.

Second, in theory, together you and your ex-spouse determine where your children reside and for how long in each home. If you cannot decide, the court will decide for you or will strongly suggest mediation to help in your decision making. For example, in Belinda and Michael Mathison's case, the placement of daughter Susan when she was young was not much different from Belinda having sole custody. Susan lived with her mother and visited her father every other weekend. As Susan grew older, she spent more time with her father, and now, as a teenager, she spends a month during the summer with her dad, plus every other weekend. Each time a change was made in Susan's visitation with her father, Belinda wisely recorded it with family court.

"What should we take into consideration when deciding placement of our children?"

Remember, you and your ex-spouse are the ones who wanted the divorce. And in its wake, the main goal is to help your children adjust easily to the changes divorce brings. Although there are a host of things parents should consider when deciding placement of their children, some of the most obvious are:

1. *Which parent was the primary caregiver?* Don't increase your child's stress by requiring them to be away from their previous primary caregiver for too long. Of course, a change in schedule will be required, but be sensitive to the child's adjustment period.
2. *Which parent has the most flexible work schedule?* This parent may be the best candidate for primary placement, because they will be the one to most often participate in carpools or pick up the children from school should they become sick.
3. *At which parent's home will the children be most comfortable?* Of course, a child would rather stay in their own room with familiar surroundings, but there are times this may not be possible. For a while, divorce makes everyone uncomfortable.

Annette Becker and her husband, Jim, decided they would attempt joint custody, with Annette retaining primary custody of Peter, eight, and Kayla, four. Annette and the children moved from the home she and Jim shared for ten years into a condominium around the block. The decision for Annette to leave the home rather than Jim was based on two factors. One, the couple had two large dogs and their home had a huge backyard for the animals. Renting another home with two children and two large dogs was almost impossible in the neighborhood in which Annette chose to relocate.

Two, Jim was a master carpenter, running a cabinet business from their home. His tools were set up in the garage and were difficult to move. But after three months of trying to adjust, Annette realized the children could not be comfortable in a condominium. Although each had a room of their own, there was no place to play and the children missed the dogs. Plus, they were constantly complaining that they were bored.

It was decided that Annette would move from the condominium into a house, but this would take three more months because she had signed a six-month lease. For the remaining three months, the children moved back into their old home. Jim became the primary caregiver until Annette secured another residence, and then their original placement agreement would stand.

"Is there a suggested placement percentage if joint custody is chosen?"

When deciding upon joint custody placement, according to a variety of attorneys nationwide, the ratio of placement most commonly used is 80/20. Eighty percent to the mother, 20 percent to the father, but this is not written in stone and can be designed to fit your family's needs.

Joint Custody Doesn't Guarantee an End to Custody Wars

Although joint custody may appear to be a less drastic custody solution than sole custody and not quite as liberal a custody solution as joint physical custody, there are aspects of joint custody that may present a problem.

"My ex and I have joint custody of the children. I have them 70 percent of the time. I have just married for the second time and my new spouse lives in another state. At the time of my remarriage, I was planning to move with my children. Is it possible I will not be permitted to take my children with me?"

"I hate to say it," says Barbara Kuehn, a family law attorney who has handled such cases for almost ten years, "but I see it all the time. Parents are so concerned about winning that they don't see what they are doing to their children."

A final divorce decree lists the child custody and visitation schedule for both parents. If your original divorce decree states that your ex-spouse is to have the children 30 percent of the time and that you may not move the children out of the area, you may not take them out of the state. Your alternatives are:

1. Leave the children behind with your ex-spouse, and set up a different visitation schedule.
2. Work out an agreement with your ex that allows you to take the kids with you but also allows them to spend the allotted amount of time with their other parent. This is why you hear of children living during the school year with one parent and the summer with another.

If you plan to move out of state after your divorce, you may still retain joint custody, but the primary placement of your children will be the big question. Again, taking into consideration that all custody decisions are decided *in the best interest of the child* and taking for granted that both parents have been found to be equally fit, the court will look for the least disruptive answer for placement. Instead of a custody battle because the type of custody was easily decided, you may have a placement battle, because both parents want the kids to live with them. In such cases, there are no pat answers. Final placement cannot be predicted because parent evaluations must be made and then reported to the court, and also because of the parents' inability to decide upon placement beforehand, the final decision will be made by a judge or officer of the court. Unless, of course, the parents are unselfish and make the placement decision with their children's welfare in mind, not on which parent "wins."

"Three years ago, my ex-wife left me and our two children. We divorced and have joint custody of the kids, but they have always lived with me. Now and then we would hear from her, but she was suffering from a midlife crisis and went off to find herself. She has since remarried and is now expecting another child. Recently, she petitioned the court and received a change in primary placement of our two kids. How could this happen?"

"Custody is not an exact science," family law attorney, Kuehn, explains. "Pure and simple, I think the reason this happened was gender bias. The mother remarried, had a change of heart, displayed sufficient regret, and convinced the court she should regain primary placement. I doubt this would have happened if the roles were reversed and the father had abandoned his wife and children.

"And in this case I believe the decision was to the detriment of the kids. They had been living with their father and flourishing for the last three years. The oldest child was only six when her mother left. Now she is nine. She barely knows her mother and feels completely disoriented. She is talking suicide because she is so confused. And when the mother was confronted with her child's depression, her response was, 'I'm going to make her love me like a daughter should love her mother.'"

Who Owns the Kids?

"Why should I bother even trying to see my son?" asks David Zuniga, thirty-six-year-old father from Amarillo, Texas. "Nothing I say matters, anyway. [My ex] acts like she owns Ben and I'm just an occasional visitor who complicates her life. All she wants is the child support payments. She doesn't care if I see Ben or not."

After divorce, it is sometimes difficult to see through the angry feelings you have for your ex-spouse, but we have to remember that it is the children who suffer when they don't interact with a healthy, caring parent. He may not be your choice for a mate, but he is your child's parent and without that healthy interaction, your child suffers.

David Zuniga's ex-wife, Rachelle, realized this after their nine-year-old son, Ben, began to suddenly have trouble sleeping through the night. She and David had been divorced for two years and had joint custody of Ben, when Rachelle decided to remarry. When a date was set for her remarriage, Rachelle simply stopped promoting visits between father and son.

"I was the one who set the times and dates for David to see Ben. He always showed up, but he never called to make dates to see his son on his own. If I didn't call, he didn't see him," she says. "So when I decided to remarry, Ben now had a brother and a sister and a chance for a real family."

But rather than assimilate easily into the new family, Ben began to lose sleep. Rachelle was confused. "I knew Ben liked my fiancé and his kids. That wasn't it. Why, when we had a chance for real happiness, was he losing sleep?"

Through counseling, it was discovered Ben did like his mother's fiancé and children. He did want to become an active member of the new family, but he also wanted to stay close to his dad. He needed interaction with his father and feared that if his mother remarried, he would never see his father again.

"If I knew Rachelle was waiting for me to call Ben, I would have called him every day! I thought that's the way she wanted it! She always made it so difficult for me to see him," David recalls. "And then when this new guy came into the picture, it didn't matter what I said, anyway."

Rachelle and David had always been at odds, so discussion was difficult, but none of this came to light until Ben had trouble sleeping and a counselor was called. Because they had joint custody of Ben, both parents took an active part in the decision to call a counselor. It took the counselor only one session to discover Ben's problem was merely his parent's lack of communication. One more session with David and Rachelle alone convinced David he had to take a more active role in his son's life. Rachelle and David developed a more organized visitation style, and now Ben is back to his old self.

This is a perfect example of how the joint custody solution almost failed, because of the poor communication skills of the participating parents. It was not the fault of joint custody but how the parents approached it. David took for granted what Rachelle wanted, and rather than make waves, he waited for her to make the visitation arrangements. Rachelle perceived the situation differently. She thought David didn't care enough to see Ben, and when she became interested in someone else, she played down the interaction with the biological father and reinforced interaction with her fiancé. The one to truly suffer was Ben.

"Do I have to pay child support, even if we share custody?"

Child support is not based on the custody arrangement but on the needs of the child. If you make more money than your ex-spouse and he/she needs the financial help to raise your child, the courts will order you to pay child support no matter what form of custody is chosen.

"When is joint custody not the proper custody solution?"

Michelle and John Mahoney divorced in 1997. Michelle had been diagnosed the year before with severe depression, and her husband, unable to deal with her illness, filed for divorce. It seemed Michelle, under the guidance of her doctor, was trying to find the proper antidepressant for her body chemistry. Many of the prescribed drugs caused extreme drowsiness and her judgment seemed impaired. Friends and neighbors reported that Michelle let Isiah, their three-year-old son, cook his own lunch on the stove because she was too listless to move, and when John was at work during the day, Isiah's diapers went unchanged.

Michelle did not want the divorce and requested joint custody. She wanted to be consulted before all decisions were made and desired a liberal visitation schedule. Initially, John agreed, but when he called Michelle one night to discuss a disciplinary tactic, she appeared so groggy from her medication that she was unable to carry on the conversation. John became alarmed, and since the divorce was not yet final, he decided to sue for sole custody of Isiah. When this case was reviewed, the court determined that until Michelle's medication was regulated, John would be awarded sole custody. When Michelle's doctor felt the correct medication had been found to deal with her depression, the custody issue could be reopened. Michelle, of course, was not happy but had to abide by the court's decision.

Another example of when joint custody may not have been the proper solution is the case of Erin and William Campos. They were married for the last five years of their fourteen-year relationship and had four children, ages six to thirteen.

Erin was raised in a severely dysfunctional family and was

physically abused as a child. As an adult she became addicted to crack cocaine, which made her unpredictable. At times, she flew into uncontrollable rages, and because she knew of no way to discipline her children other than the way she had been disciplined, she began to physically abuse them, all the while threatening their lives if they ever told their father. Not knowing of the physical abuse or drug addiction, William filed for divorce for reasons of his own and moved out of the home. Erin convinced William that joint custody was the right answer and that the children should remain in the home.

After William left, Erin became even more unpredictable. The children were confused by their mother's irrational behavior. They were never sure how she would react when they came home from school. Would she greet them with a smile or be upstairs fast asleep? Would she hug them or fly off the handle and beat them with a hairbrush? They were afraid to say a word because of their mother's threats.

Although Erin tried to hide her addiction, her older children, aware of the telltale signs of drug addiction as a result of a school DARE class, confronted their mother. She categorically denied her problem. However, when a friend of the children was disciplined with a spanking while playing at Erin's house, the parent's child contacted William and everything was brought out into the open. William then filed an emergency transfer placement, and the children moved in with him. He also petitioned family court for sole custody. Erin was granted supervised visitation and ordered into drug rehab and counseling.

Joint custody is not the correct solution if there is concern for the mental or physical welfare of your children. If there is a history of mental illness, drug or sexual abuse, undermining the other parent (which would constitute mental abuse if the child were caught in the middle), defiance of the law, actively interfering with visitation, or anything that would lead you to believe that constant interaction with your ex-spouse would be detrimental to your children, consider sole custody.

"If we choose joint custody, may both my ex-spouse and I sign legal papers for our children?"

Yes, that is one of the benefits of joint custody. Parents have equal rights, specifically in legal matters, and you both still *feel* like parents. If your child wants to marry before the age of eighteen or join the armed forces, then because you have joint custody, either parent's consent is enough. But it is important to stay in close communication with your ex-spouse, or the joint custody solution could be used against you.

Ruby Garcia's parents were divorced when she was eleven. They decided that joint custody was the best solution. Ruby lived with her mother and visited her father regularly when she was young, but her father was in the navy and was now stationed in another state, Hawaii, and it was more difficult for Ruby to see her father on a regular basis.

Upon graduation at age seventeen, Ruby went to visit her father, with aspirations of returning home to California in a month to attend a local university. But plans changed. Ruby was attracted to the life of a naval officer and decided to join the service in Hawaii. Her mother, furious with her decision, demanded she return to California immediately. Her serviceman father supported her decision and signed Ruby's admission papers. Even though she was not eighteen, she was in the navy now, prompting a huge vendetta between Ruby's mother and father.

This decision worked out fine for Ruby in the long run, but if ex-spouses are fighting and don't agree, you can see how a joint custody solution may be used to simply get back at the ex-spouse rather than benefit the child. Remember, the child's welfare must always come first.

"If we couldn't get along when we were married, how can we get along well enough to successfully raise our children together after divorce?"

Critics of this custody solution often raise this very question, which is why many of them view joint custody as an impossible solution. Joint custody takes a lot of soul-searching, pride-swallowing, and tongue-biting to make it work. Sounds painful, doesn't it? While convalescing from deep wounds is often painful, if you can keep your focus on problem solving and put your children first, joint custody may be difficult but not impossible. Studies show that because parents who chose joint custody spend so much time searching for answers and coordinating schedules, they *learn* to get along far better after divorce than parents who chose sole custody. It is unfortunate that this happens only once the marriage is over.

But don't be misled into thinking this custody solution is for everyone. On the contrary, it is for a select few who are determined to develop a collaborative relationship for the sake of their children and raise their children together—divorced or not. If, after your divorce, anger and revenge rule your behavior toward your ex-spouse, it is doubtful joint custody is your solution.

"What are some of the drawbacks of joint custody?"

Maintaining two households is expensive, and in order for children to see each parent as often as necessary, shuttling children here and there can be distressing. The main disadvantage to joint custody is not the concept itself but the frailties of the parents at-tempting this arrangement. You may not live with your ex-spouse, but if joint custody is approached properly, you will speak to them each time something monumental happens to your child. If your child wins an award or is caught stealing, it's all the same, and if joint custody is chosen, it is the obligation of both parents to include their ex-spouse in making all decisions for their children. If you cannot honestly make this commitment, joint custody is probably not a good solution.

"I never wanted joint custody of our children. It was the court's bright idea. I wanted sole custody, and I plan to make my ex's life miserable until the custody order is changed."

These days, many states award joint custody as a standard proce-dure, understanding that both the father and mother are capable parents and can provide their children equal emotional and finan-cial support. Your children will suffer if you take out your anger on your ex-spouse. Plus, if you interfere with the court order too much, for example, you prevent your ex-spouse from seeing the children or you don't pay ordered child support, your ex can peti-tion the court on the grounds that you are interfering with their visitation, and they may gain sole custody at that point.

But there's good news. It seems joint custody solution sets a stage for conflict resolution. Professionals report that when di-vorced parents share custody of their children, they are more likely to seek counseling or mediation to deal with their anger and disagreements instead of depriving their ex-spouse of parent-ing their child. Another important positive in favor of joint cus-tody is that it has been found that parents who share custody after divorce and see their children on a regular basis take a more active role in their children's upbringing and are more likely to stay up-to-date on their child support payments.

Consistent Discipline

One of the most difficult battles fought by all parents is the one to maintain consistency in disciplining. The bantering of "Mom said I can" when Dad said no is not a new concept. This can be easily overcome when everyone lives under the same roof and love and affection balance the discord, but when you have two divorced parents who both believe they are head of the household, it's not as easy. Mom could be angry about Dad being a little late on his child support payments, or Dad could be a little miffed that Mom was late in returning the children. Just to prove a point, Mom allows the children to do something she knows Dad will not like. Then, to add insult to injury, she tells the children not to say anything to their father. This is a heavy burden to lay on the shoulders of little children, and eventually such behavior backfires.

Brian, a six-year-old whose parents have been divorced for the last three years, lived with his mother 70 percent of the time. He saw his father, Jay, who lived in the next city, at least two days a week. At their last visit, Brian was nervous and Jay could see the difference in his son's behavior, but he could have never predicted how simply asking what was wrong could have prompted his son to tears. "At that point, Brian became hysterical and I feared the worst. The first thing that went through my head was that my child had been abused and because I wasn't with him all the time, I couldn't protect him. My reaction was probably far more extreme than it needed to be," Jay says.

What was the problem? Brian's mother, Cathy, had picked Brian up from school early for some ice cream. It was a surprise and his mother told the school Brian had a dentist appointment. Brian was to tell no one of their secret. Brian's response was, "Not even Daddy?" and Brian's mother, trying to keep the day special, said, "Not even Daddy." Brian then thought he was doing something wrong, and the next time he saw his father, he was quiet and withdrawn. He was protecting his mother.

On his next visit with his dad, Brian spent the first hour on the verge of tears. That's when Brian "slipped." He told on his mommy. Brian's father became angry—the exact reaction this poor little boy feared—not because his ex-wife had picked up their son for a special afternoon of ice cream but because she told him not to tell his father. This innocent act mushroomed into a huge problem. It prompted Jay to be concerned that there were other, more important instances when the truth had been kept from him.

Brian's mother and father had the presence of mind to go to a mediator rather than allow the discord to accelerate, but that was not Jay's first reaction. "I wanted to tell Brian how stupid I thought his mother was, but what would that do? In the long run, it would make Brian feel worse and me, too. I know Brian's mother very well. I was married to her for seven years. She just hadn't picked the right words to explain their special day. But I was so angry at the time that I had to have a third party in the room before I spoke to her. That was a hundred dollar argument."

The mediator charged Brian's parents for the session, but it was a hundred dollars well spent. Small misunderstandings undermine the great intentions of joint custody. Brian's parents did their best to keep this misunderstanding away from their son and continued to work on their communication.

"Mediation has been far more effective for us than counseling," Jay maintains. "We found that counselors look for the deep-seated reasons as to why you do the things you do. That's well and good, but the truth is, I'm divorced from Cathy. What went wrong is in the past. I'm looking for immediate answers to effectively raise my child. I don't want to take six months to figure out that Cathy or I have deep-seated anger, which propels us to undermine something. A mediator asks us to work out a solution in a session or two."

Although Jay's attitude may not be the popular one, his ex-wife, Cathy, agrees with him. "We know stupid stuff like our misunderstanding can drive you crazy and eat away at you. The next twenty times I saw Jay, I would be angry. And, of course, Brian could tell. What would my anger really do to Jay? Brian would be the one I was hurting. Jay and I split the hundred dollars, worked it out, and then went on. If you look at how much time and energy our mediator saved us, it was cheap."

Joint Custody After Divorce Parent Panel

"Why did you choose this type of custody agreement?"

Of all the parents polled for this chapter, both Belinda and Michael Mathison summarize it best. "Because even though we could not live with each other, we both loved our children and wanted to take an active part in their lives."

"How is joint custody working for you now?"

BELINDA MATHISON: "In the beginning, joint custody was rather trying. I felt the baby belonged to me and almost resented Michael's interaction. Secretly, I was afraid if I let Michael have too much say in the upbringing of *my* child, I would lose her. I knew fathers were often getting custody and since I initiated the divorce. . .

"I came to see that Susan wasn't just my child, and when I accepted that fact, a whole new world opened up to me. I not only let Michael see her more often, which was his right as her father, but I started discussing things with him just as I should have from the beginning when we agreed to joint custody. Now that Sue is older, I am grateful to have Michael's support. She is very headstrong and almost too much for me to handle by myself. It's nice to have someone to call when things get tough."

JANN BLACKSTONE-FORD: "In my own experience I, too, was uncomfortable giving up custody of my daughter when my ex-husband and I divorced years ago. In 1983, joint custody was a new concept. Of course people were doing it, but it wasn't as common as the mother receiving sole custody and the father receiving visitation. Being newly single and striving for my own independence, I did not release the control over the situation I felt I needed. Rather than address problems or ask my ex-husband's opinion when making decisions, I simply avoided conflict and Annie's stepfather became more active in her life.

This is a dangerous cop-out when choosing joint custody as your solution, and a common mistake. When you divorce, you are no longer one family unit. You are two separate entities. Unfortunately, the parent that has physical custody of the child is usually the one who feels they are in control. But that is not the essence of the joint custody solution. Your agreement is to openly discuss all decisions concerning your child, to make important decisions together in the best interest of the child. I found joint custody to be an ongoing learning process, and my performance improved as time went on."

"How did this custody choice affect your children?"

RACHELLE SMITHSON, formerly Rachelle Zuniga: "I was tired of fighting and being confrontational, but I wanted to be a family. When I decided to remarry I realized I had that chance, so I slowly stopped promoting Ben's visits with his father. It seemed less complicated that way. Now I see reinforcing a strong relationship with his father made Ben a much more stable person, and I am embarrassed by my behavior."

JANN BLACKSTONE-FORD: "Again, as Annie grew older, I watched as she began to manifest the same problems and personality traits with which her father had struggled for years. Discussing her feelings was very difficult for her, and I was also afraid she was battling depression, just as her father had suffered as an adult. The logical candidate with whom to discuss the problem was her father, but even though we had joint custody of Annie, our communication was strained. The love of our daughter, however, allowed us to move past our own anger and frustration to make the proper decisions for Annie. This summer, she is spending six weeks with her father. I have to admit, I find it amusing that her depression lifted as soon as report cards were received and she was not grounded for her grades. But we are keeping a close eye on her should the depression resume and counseling becomes necessary."

"Would you change anything if you could?"

RACHELLE SMITHSON: "I wish I would have seen from the beginning how important consistent interaction is between father and son. Instead, I forced my son into counseling because of my inability to communicate with his father. I knew intellectually that interaction was important, which was why we chose joint custody to begin with, but then I got involved with my own life and wanted Ben to assimilate into it so much that I forgot my responsibility to support his biological father's interaction. Although I didn't do this on purpose, I am now embarrassed by my insensitivity."

BETH WILKINSON: "I wish we could have figured out our solution of my moving closer to my ex-husband sooner. I spent two summers without my kids, and they were the longest months of my life. But, it was where we were in our communication. David was not ready to suggest the move sooner than he did, and I wasn't ready to accept moving as an answer to our visitation problems. You just don't think you will have to stay that close to your ex-husband after a divorce. I thought he was out of my life, and we would raise the kids together over the telephone. It doesn't work that way."

BEATRICE PUBLIC LIBRARY
BEATRICE, NEBR. 68310

CHAPTER FIVE

Joint Custody with Joint Physical Custody

"A pessimist sees the difficulty in every opprtunity, an optimist sees the opportunity in every difficulty."
—Sir Winston Churchill

Joint physical custody is a special custody solution. Although more and more divorcing parents are attempting this type of arrangement, it is not for everyone. "I would like to caution parents who believe joint physical custody is the easiest answer to staying close to your children after divorce," says Donald Uslan, a psychotherapist from Seattle, who often counsels families that chose joint physical custody. "Joint physical custody only works if the parents truly put the child first when making decisions. The constant interaction with one's ex-spouse can be exhausting. I know of parents who chose joint physical custody merely because they were afraid to let their ex-spouse have one extra minute of time with the kids, and with the courts granting them equal time, they felt they had won a victory against their ex-spouse. Check your motives. That is not the reason to attempt it. Your children are watching and learning from every move you make."

"What is the difference between joint custody and joint physical custody?"

Joint custody allows you to share the responsibilities of raising your children with your ex-spouse after divorce, whereas joint *physical* custody takes this one step further: This arrangement says both parents also have physical custody of the kids, that is, the kids live 50 percent of the time with Mom and 50 percent of the time with Dad. How the parents achieve this 50-percent placement order is at their own discretion. Some parents choose to have their children live at one parent's house for the first six months of the year and then the other parent's house the last six months. Some families switch every other week. Some choose every two weeks or every other month. Whatever your approach to your children's placement, the child is required to spend an equal amount of time with each parent, but you may design the placement to accommodate your lifestyle.

The jury is still out concerning the psychological effects on children who live within a joint physical custody solution. Some therapists view the constant interaction with both parents as a stabilizing force in a child's upbringing—far more stabilizing than sole custody, where the emotional relationship between noncustodial parent and child is constantly disrupted by the child returning to the authority and home of the custodial parent. In my first book, *My Parent's Are Divorced, Too*, the young authors, who happen to be my biological daughter from my first marriage and my stepchildren, tell the reader how confused they were when their parents began divorce proceedings, and explain that the joint physical custody approach was helpful in their adjustment. However, critics of this custody solution feel the constant moving back and forth is detrimental and prolongs the child's adjustment period after divorce. Not having one place to call their own and no single bedroom where they can stash their stuff may make them feel as if they do not belong anywhere.

When Joint Physical Custody Works

Sally Williams of Livermore, California, disagrees that children do not fare well in the joint physical custody environment. "My children are thriving because we chose joint physical custody, and the fact that they have a room at their father's house and a room at my house only reinforces that they have an active place in both our families. But, I have to admit, years ago, when I told my friends I was going to agree to Charlie having joint physical custody of our children, Megan, seven, and Jack, three, they told me I was crazy. My daughter was already suffering from psycho-somatic aches and pains because of our divorce. My friends cautioned me, saying that if the kids went back and forth, it would just be asking for problems. Plus, at the time, few divorced fathers were taking such an active role in their children's lives after divorce. Friends cautioned me and suggested that Charlie would not show the consistency needed to raise healthy kids."

"But I was adamant about the joint custody solution," says Charlie Ford, a general contractor who also lives in Livermore. "I adored my children and wanted to see them every day. I had the type of lifestyle where I could take off from work when I wanted and pick my daughter up from school if I had to. I wanted to be there. I did not want to be a weekend father."

Charlie and Sally decided the placement of their children would be 50/50, and within that framework they have accommodated the children as they have grown older. "Originally, the children went back and forth every few days," Sally explains. "This was as much for us as it was for the children, but it was difficult for them to stay organized, and Megan often left her homework or her library books at the other parent's house, so for her, going back and forth so often was unsettling. Steven, who was so young, adjusted quickly."

"Then when I remarried," Charlie adds, "the constant switching back and forth was just too disruptive. So we tried every other week. We switched on Fridays, and the children seemed to thrive with the more structured schedule."

As this story implies, for joint physical custody to work, you must live close to your ex-spouse. When the children are very young, if you choose the six months at one parent's, six months at the other parent's home, this may not be necessary. But as your children grow older and start school, to guarantee consistency, parents must live nearby.

When Sally remarried, her friends again expressed concern. "We live in a small town, and at first, when we all showed up to a Little League game, our friends feared there would be problems, but it never bothered me. Then when Jeff and Charlie both coached Megan's softball team, tongues were wagging!"

Jeff Williams, Sally's new husband, adds, "Why cause problems? The kids didn't want the divorce, Charlie and Sally did. They were doing this switching back and forth for years before I got into the picture. My job was to support my wife's decision. And the children seemed happy. Frankly, I think the going back and forth made the children more accepting of me when I married their mother."

Psychotherapist Uslan confirms this view. "Of course there are exceptions to every rule, but more often than not, I have found that children raised in a joint physical custody environment learn to be more accommodating as people. Because they live in two different places, they readily learn to deal with change."

So with the help of their new spouses, Charlie and Sally continued this every other week switch for eight years, or until Megan and Steven turned sixteen and twelve, respectively, and began to complain. "By the time I would get settled, it was time to leave again," recalls Megan. "We had to do something else."

Problem Solving When Choosing Joint Physical Custody

To ensure success when choosing joint physical custody, the two households must establish an equitable way to problem-solve if a disagreement arises. Sally, Charlie, and their new spouses simply meet in a nonhostile environment, for them, the local pizza parlor, and hash it out. They call it, for want of a better title, a "Parent Discussion."

"The key here," says Janet, Charlie's new wife, "is that everyone wants this lifestyle to work. Rather than spend a lot of time name-calling and blaming each other for things, the parents—as the kids refer to us as a group—really look for solutions that will accommodate everyone, but especially the kids. If Megan feels uncomfortable going back and forth every week, then we will try every two weeks. We roll with the punches. Our agenda is the kids, not which parent has more control or who won this time."

An aspect of the parent discussion that all four adults agree on is that they meet first, establish policy, then as a united front introduce the idea to the children. "The one thing I vowed I would never do again is fight in front of the kids," says Sally. "I saw what that did to my children. So, if there is a disagreement or something needs to be discussed, the parents meet, come to some conclusion and then talk to the children. I will not upset my children again with screaming and confusion."

Professionals agree with this approach. "The goal of any good parent is to minimize their children's confusion after a divorce," Uslan says. "Charlie and Sally are doing a good job giving their children a solid base with which to face the uncertainties of life after divorce . . . attempting to appear as a united front is a difficult task when married . . . when divorced it may be almost impossible . . . but it is a noble goal. Children of divorce fare far better when they are confident their parents are in control."

This can be seen in the case of Jackie Baily, whose parents divorced when she was seven. Jackie's mother, Melissa, was upset about the divorce and cried often during the first few months of adjustment after the separation. Jackie perceived this crying as a lack of control and believed she was now responsible for the emotional well-being of not only herself but that of her little brother, Andy. Jackie fell behind in school and had difficulty sleeping at night because of the great burden she was now carrying. A seven-year-old's perception of crying meant her mother had lost control.

Jackie's teacher noticed a drop in the quality of her schoolwork and after discussing the situation with Melissa, suggested the school counselor be consulted. One session helped Jackie see that crying meant her mother was sad but not out of control and still fully capable of taking care of her and Andy. Additional reassurances from Jackie's mother, and a few less tears in front of the kids, helped put her daughter back on track.

New Partners

"My ex-husband has a new girlfriend and she's sleeping at the house. I think it's too soon. What do I do?"

Talk to him about it. You have joint physical custody of the children. He should be expecting a call. But, more importantly, this is the type of thing you must discuss and agree on *before* you attempt this custody agreement. If you don't want to have to explain anything to your ex-spouse, joint physical custody is not for you.

"My husband and I were married five months ago. He and his ex-wife have joint physical custody of the kids, which means they live with us for a week then live with her for a week. When we are not home, his ex-wife sometimes comes into our house to collect toys or clothing that were forgotten. This makes me uncomfortable."

While sole custody and visitation rarely put you in the position where you may have to interact with your new spouse's ex-partner other than an occasional phone call, joint physical custody introduces a degree of familiarity that may initially make you uncomfortable. But remember, you are raising the kids *together*. That means everyone will be interacting with your child—exes and new spouses of both divorcing parents. You may be talking to his ex-wife every day, and with all the traveling back and forth, toys will be left behind or the laundry may get mixed up and you will have unfamiliar clothes in your washer.

I remember attending a school play in which my daughter, Annie, had the lead. It was a big deal for our family, and my husband's ex-wife brought their kids to see the play. It was her week and she was supporting the relationship the children had built as stepsister and brother. I was sitting next to her, and as we chatted about the kid's recent accomplishments, I pulled up my pant leg and said, "Hey, do these socks look familiar? I think they are yours." It was a joke, to make light of our situation, but she got me. She pulled up her pant leg to show me her socks. "I've never seen these, either." The socks were mine. While transferring clothes from one house to another, my stepdaughter, Melanie, had mixed up socks, underwear, even the good towels from the guest bathroom.

The obvious answer here is boundaries must be established and respected. An open door policy may be healthy for the children when joint physical custody is chosen, but the adults need their privacy.

Deb and Doug Minor of Darian, Connecticut, have an easy suggestion for the problem of retrieving additional clothing or toys when the parents are not home. "My children have a key to both my home and their father's. If they have left something behind and their dad is not home, I take them to the house and *let them go in and get it*. Although I was married to their dad for quite a while and he is still living in the home that we originally purchased together, he has been remarried for quite a while. Out of respect for their union, I would never enter their home uninvited." Deb goes on to explain that she regards this as a good lesson for her children. "My parents taught me to treat people the way I would like to be treated. When they were teaching me this they did not say, *except your ex-husband and his wife*. If we are going to successfully share physical custody, my kids need to learn respect for all the parents concerned. I would hope my ex would treat me with the same concern—for our children's sake."

Deb's attitude is probably one of the reasons she and her ex-husband have been so successful at the joint physical custody solution. However, if you anticipate unannounced visits from your ex-spouse or mixed-up laundry will make you uncomfortable, rethink the joint physical custody solution because this is bound to happen.

Consistency in Discipline

"What if our child gets into trouble and the rules are not the same at my ex's house?"

Consistency on all levels is the key for success in joint physical custody. If the rules change whenever the child leaves a parent's home, he may become confused as to who is right and who is wrong. Without knowing it, the parents are again pitting themselves against each other and asking their children to take sides.

If the punishment at one house for disobeying is no television for a week, then ideally, punishment at the other house should be the same. Taking this one step further, if a child is on restriction at one house and their time at that house is over, then the restriction should continue at the other house.

"Oh, the kids try to play us one against the other," laughs Charlie Ford. "I used to hear 'but Mom lets us do it' all the time. Janet nipped that one in the bud. She just called Sally and asked her what policy was at her house so we could reinforce it at ours. They discussed it, came to a conclusion, and the kids know they can't do that anymore because someone will be on the phone to get the story straight. It has been a long process, but we work at it."

"We have had our ups and downs," agrees Sally. "When we first attempted joint physical custody years ago, there were times when Charlie and I were so angry at each other we couldn't even be in the same room. We would write letters back and forth because we couldn't talk to each other. We were divorced, trying to raise our children together and we could not discuss a thing. The change came when we truly began to put the needs of the children first. You can't allow your anger for each other to control your decision making for your children. You have to let the love you both have for your children be your guide."

"What are some of the unanticipated drawbacks of the joint custody with joint physical custody solution?"

Aside from the psychological effects on the children (on which professionals do not agree), other unique problems arise as time passes.

When Louise and Donald Pearlstein divorced, they agreed to joint physical custody of their two children, Marsha and Brett. After two years of successfully sharing custody and the children going back and forth between the two homes, Donald married Frances, who had a seven-year-old daughter, Ellen, from a previous marriage. Ellen, Marsha, and Brett became fast friends and delighted in calling each other brother and sisters. Both Frances and Donald reinforced this feeling, but a problem arose because of it.

Marsha and Brett lived at Donald's house for a week, then went to their mother's house for a week. When they returned to their father's house they brought along little gifts their mother had given them before they left. Seven-year-old Ellen wanted to know why her sister and brother received gifts, but she had not. Ellen did not understand that the children's mother, unhappy that it was her children's time to return to their father's, bought them little gifts to remember her by. But this gesture, no matter how unselfish in origin, confused the issue when the children returned to their father's.

When confronted with the problem, Louise was resentful, explaining it was her right to buy her own kids presents whenever she wanted. This was true, agreed Donald, but he explained the situation he was facing with little Ellen. Louise held her ground until she realized she was giving the presents to her children to allay her own guilt about the divorce, and each time the children left, she had to address that guilt. The gifts eased her pain, but Marsha and Brett were not really benefiting from the gifts, and Ellen was definitely being hurt.

"When you attempt the joint custody solution, you have to accept everything dished onto your plate," explains Louise. "Ellen was not in the original picture, but when Donald and I accepted the responsibility of joint physical custody, we were agreeing that we would support each other's decisions concerning the children, even after the divorce. The children now had a stepsister, and looking at the problem from that standpoint, I understood what Donald was saying. I had to make my decisions based on the entire picture, not just my desires."

It was decided that all toys, excluding special birthday or Christmas presents, would stay at the home in which they had been given.

A year after this problem was overcome, another dilemma arose. Frances became pregnant. Now there would be another child added to the family, and Donald, Frances, Marsha, Ellen, and Brett rejoiced at the prospect of this little bundle further joining their family. The new baby was raised as a sister to the three older children, and when little Haley was old enough to realize her older brother and sister were leaving for a week, she became hysterical. She didn't understand why they were leaving her. To add to the problem, the oldest, Marsha, viewed Haley's sadness as her fault because she had to leave and felt responsible for hurting her little sister. She became despondent and withdrawn.

The family turned to counseling for Marsha. She had to address the issues that were plaguing her as a result of her little sister's sadness. Second, a more open-door policy was adopted for little Haley. If she missed her brother and sister on the weeks they were with their mother, she could simply call them. "When that didn't seem enough," Louise adds, "we invited Haley over for a tea party. She thought that was so great! We only live two miles away. It seemed so silly to make a little girl go through that."

Louise's understanding of the situation made Frances more open to her, and now they regard each other as friends. "Divorce is not easy for anyone. I thought Louise's gesture of inviting Haley over for a tea party was very unselfish, and I really appreciated it. I began to relax around her and all of a sudden we were openly discussing how to handle the kids in various situations. That little gesture changed the entire course of our relationship," states Frances.

"I may be imagining it, but it seems my five-year-old daughter takes a day to adjust when she returns from her week at her dad's house. She's crabby and doesn't like to do anything but watch TV the first day back. By the next day she's herself and ready to play, but I worry if the joint physical custody solution is really the right choice for her."

What you describe has been the observation of many parents attempting the 50/50 split and is also the reason the jury is still out concerning this solution. On one hand, some therapists believe the 50/50, Mom's house/Dad's house approach is a positive solution to dividing a child's time between divorced parents, while other therapists suggest that the going back and forth between Mom's house and Dad's house extends the child's period of adjustment after divorce.

I believe that if there is anything you can do to make your children's life happier after a divorce, you do it. In my experience, my stepchildren missed the other parent so much that the 50/50 split was the only possible solution for our family. As a result, the children have adjusted nicely. But would they have been less affected if they had stayed with their mother and their father had visitation? My stepchildren would have been, but this is not to say that this solution is the answer for your child. Only you, your ex, and your children know the answer to that.

Stay Organized

Pat and Bob Denny had another unanticipated problem when attempting the joint physical custody solution. "It is embarrassing for me to admit," says Pat, "but this is my third marriage. I have one child from my first marriage and one child from my second.

Now I have a child from this marriage, and my husband has two children from his first marriage. I had joint physical custody of both of my children from previous marriages, and he had joint physical custody of his two children. It was difficult to keep everything straight. There are a lot of parents involved in the decision making."

Although the divorce rate has leveled off in the last few years, it is still around 50 percent. This not only means lots of blended families, and as in Pat Denny's case, blended families within blended families. "It wouldn't be my choice to raise my kids like this," she says. "I have made decisions I am not proud of and if I could, I would take back many of the things I have said and done. But I can't, and now I must make the best of it."

Her only saving grace, Pat notes, is her ability to organize and prioritize. "The first thing I did was get everyone on the *same* schedule." With joint physical custody and the children coming and going, the need for a consistent schedule was obvious. "Joint physical custody is no place for egos. I was in way over my head. I just appealed to the powers that be," meaning, she called a meeting of all the parents involved—both of her ex-husbands and Bob's ex-wife—and asked for their help. "The odds of everyone working together were one in a million. All those egos and hurt feelings. But I guess everyone was feeling the strain." Together they worked out a living schedule that was equitable for everyone. "I know this sounds crazy, but we did it. We chose a restaurant because we knew no one would lose their temper in public. I showed up at the meeting with four huge desk calendars and gave one to each family. We planned as much of the year as possible together. I thank God every day that we are all as committed to all the children."

Bob Denny does not share Pat's philosophical attitude about joint physical custody. "This lifestyle is truly a test of my patience, but the kids seem to be well balanced and happy with it, and that's why we are doing it. I'm not sure if Pat's older daughter likes it as much as the younger ones. She's concerned with her clothes and where they are. She hates being at one place when her 'cool' shoes are left at the other house, but we try to accommodate everyone as much as possible. If it becomes too much, we will make a change. That's the beauty of it. We are in control, and if the kids don't seem to be thriving, we look for another solution."

A common occurrence in this type of custody solution is that the parents become so concerned about compensating for their children that the kids control both households. James Porter, the new mate of a twice-divorced mother, Connie, tells us, "My wife and her ex-husband felt terrible about getting a divorce. Their son, Jason, was not doing well with the adjustment, which made Connie and Dean afraid to make a decision or become angry with the children. No one wanted to hurt the kids any further, but the parents' guilt allowed the kids to run everything."

"I have seen this in my practice," agrees psychotherapist Uslan, "when parents allow guilt to rule the roost, so to speak. They allow their children to break the household rules because they feel so badly that their lives were disrupted by divorce. Of course, choosing joint physical custody offers new problems that may not have been an issue if the children were not being raised in two separate homes, but the reality is, the parents are divorced, and the guilt they feel must be addressed as a separate issue, not allowed to spill over into the disciplining of their children."

Two of Everything

If you choose joint physical custody as your custody solution, your children will live 50 percent of the time with you and 50 percent of the time with your ex-spouse. They now have two homes and two families that are equally important.

Two of everything was a difficult concept for Simon Michaelson of San Francisco to accept. "I was paying child support to buy my son a toothbrush at my house and a toothbrush at his mother's, clothes at my house, clothes at his mother's, but when my ex-wife wanted to buy him a bicycle for her house because she was tired of lugging it back and forth, I had to put my foot down. I couldn't afford to buy him two bikes. That was crazy."

Perhaps Michaelson's family took this concept a little too far. The reality is, most parents cannot afford to buy their children two of everything, which is where the coordination between parents becomes a necessity if joint physical custody is to work. Every child needs their own space, their own corner. Whether they have to share a room with another sibling or they are lucky enough to have their own room, arrangements must still be made to make them feel at home in both houses.

Small compensations may be all that is needed when joint physical custody is chosen, as illustrated by this story of adjustment. Donna Hepburn of Scottsdale, Arizona, recalls "My ex-husband and I were not wealthy by any means and I had to have a roommate after the divorce to make ends meet. When my son spent his two weeks of the month at my home, he had to share a room with my roommate's son, Louie, but when he was at his dad's, he had his own room. I compensated for the lack of space by lots of ceremony. I made a big deal of introducing him to Louie, showing him which side of the chest of drawers was his, these two shelves in the medicine cabinet are yours. This is your new green metal flake toothbrush. This is your space to store your stuff, and no one will bother it. That made him feel like he belonged there."

Sometimes the compensations necessary to make joint physical custody work may not be that small. Once again, Sally Williams explains a predicament she has had to face because of her initial choice of joint physical custody.

"Three years ago, my second husband was transferred to Los Angeles, four hundred miles away from our home. Because my ex-husband and I have joint physical custody of our kids, if I moved along with him, I would have to give up my joint physical custody status. The original custody agreement was 50 percent of the time with me and 50 percent of the time with my ex. This physical placement would be impossible for me if I moved four hundred miles away. I was now put in the position of choosing between my living with my husband or my children."

Sally and Jeff Williams worked out an unconventional solution that would not suit all married couples. "Jeff and I have worked out a plan where he lives four days a week in Los Angeles and three days a week at home so I can stay with my kids, but it is by no means something I want to do for much longer. It puts an incredible strain on our marriage."

But this is the type of situation you have to anticipate when considering the joint physical custody solution—how will you and your ex adjust to changes that are not relevant to you at the time of your initial decision? Develop a plan. Discuss every possible scenario from remarriage to job changes and relocation, and always keep your ex informed should something unforeseen prevent you from going through with what you agreed upon together.

"What are some of the positive aspects of joint physical custody we may not have discussed?"

Maria Garcia of Santa Fe, New Mexico, tells us that joint physical custody was the answer to her prayers. "My ex-husband and I were constantly battling. He was very controlling and felt that my place was in the home taking care of the kids . . . twenty-four hours a day, every day, no friends, just the kids. Don't get me wrong. I love my kids, but I had to leave so I could breathe!"

It is obvious that Maria and her ex-husband had some major issues to overcome in their marriage, and when those issues could not be resolved, Maria chose to leave the marriage and be on her own. "On my own with the kids," Maria interjects, "but Carlos would not allow me to have sole custody. He wanted them, too, and being that he is an excellent father, joint physical custody seemed the best answer."

Maria tells us that by choosing joint physical custody for her children, she can have a social life and be a mommy, too. "I don't mix my family life with my social life right now, so for me, sharing physical custody of my children with their dad seems the best of both worlds. When I was married, I was always a mommy. I never had a break. My husband was so controlling, I had no other life than the kids. Now, because of joint physical custody, my ex has the children for a week at a time. On my weeks with the kids, I stay home, cook dinner every night, and it is family time. On the weeks when the kids are with their father, I go out with my friends, even date occasionally, and I don't worry about a babysitter or the effects of my behavior on my children because they are with their dad. When I meet someone with whom I think I may have a future, then I will introduce him to my kids. But for now, I have my social weeks and I have my mommy weeks, and the two don't cross over."

"When is the joint physical custody solution a poor choice?"

The story of Louise and Donald Pearlstein demonstrates how much accommodation you must consider when attempting the joint physical custody solution. There are times when unanticipated problems arise, whereby you must swallow your pride and regroup for the sake of the whole, so to speak. In Louise's case, it wasn't even her child that was being affected, but because she chose to raise her children in that environment, she had to consider how her behavior was affecting the other household. If you do not feel you can be that accommodating after divorce, the joint physical custody solution may not be for you.

"We tried it," says Mitch Jefferson, a thirty-six-year-old automobile dealer from Detroit. "The kids lived at my house for a week, then Lucy's house for a week, but when I got them back, they were whiny and unruly. They had to watch television to fall asleep, something I absolutely forbade when their mother and I lived together."

The joint physical custody solution can easily become a battleground if both parents do not cooperate. If there are unresolved issues, the necessity to be in constant communication with each other will not heal those old wounds. "It got to the point where I was so angry at Lucy I started calling her names in front of the kids, and I didn't even know I was doing it. One day my daughter started crying because I called her mommy an idiot, and I knew we had to change something. Then James started to wet the bed. He hadn't wet the bed for two years. At first I thought he was reacting to the divorce itself, but while discussing it, our counselor said no."

"James was adjusting as well as could be expected to his parents no longer living together," his counselor reports. "I believe his parents' constant bickering in front of him and the inconsistency between households were upsetting him. As soon as the fighting stopped and he knew what to expect, James was back to his old self."

"Although I wanted to be there all the time, I couldn't take the constant battles. I felt like Lucy was trying to sabotage my authority, and since we didn't live together, what could I say? It was not a healthy environment for the kids," Mitch says.

After six months of attempting to raise their children in a joint physical custody environment, he wanted a change. "Believe it or not, I was the one to suggest the change. We still have joint custody, and Lucy discusses everything concerning the kids with me, but they now live with Lucy full time. My youngest is only four, and I thought she should be with her mother. I see them at least every weekend and sometimes for dinner in the middle of the week. We work around our schedules. When they get older, we may adjust the situation, but for now, for the sake of the children, the fighting had to stop."

"I'm at my wit's end," confides Valerie Stephenson, a divorced mother attempting the joint physical custody solution. "My son, Randy, hates living for extended periods at his dad's. He feels his stepmother is mean and controlling. Randy's only ten years old, and he has anxiety attacks and trouble sleeping when he anticipates having to return to his father's. Two months at my home, then two months at his dad's is just too long of a stretch at one time."

Valerie and her ex-husband, Jim, are legally divorced, but their custody arrangement is still in question. Neither Valerie nor Jim want to fight this out in court, but attempting to take it on themselves could be dangerous to their child. If Randy is truly reacting as strongly to the moving back and forth as Valerie states, he should be observed by a professional, and the professional's recommendation should be taken seriously. And Valerie should take note. Just because Jim doesn't want to go to court doesn't mean the case won't be heard by a judge. If she is concerned for her son's mental health, and her ex-husband does not agree on custody placement, she can initiate a court proceeding. When the courts get involved, and there is a disagreement between parents concerning custody, a formal parent evaluation is often ordered. A therapist will interview everyone concerned, and if Randy is truly affected psychologically, the therapist's recommendation will reflect that.

"Jim is adamant about sharing physical custody of Randy. He says it's important for a son to grow up with his father around, which I agree, but there is another concern. Jim's wife has told him that if Randy lives with them six months out of the year they will be able to use him as a tax write-off. He doesn't seem to care about Randy's mental health, just whether he is eligible for an additional tax break." Jim's tax break could be in question. If you are in a similar situation, check with a credible tax consultant before you do anything.

The gauge if any custody solution is successful is how well your children fare in the environment. If your child appears even-tempered, sleeps well, does well in school, and most of all, *tells you they are happy*, then that's the solution for you. If, like Randy, your child appears sullen, cries at the drop of a hat, becomes "clingy" when you are separated for normal periods of time, and *tells you how unhappy they are* with the placement arrangement, it's time to reassess your custody placement agreement.

The court's final decision will always be in the best interest of the child. The court will hear Jim's desire for equal placement for Randy and note it, but if it's not in Randy's best interest, the court will make another ruling.

"My ex-husband and I have joint physical custody of our kids. They live with us every other week. My problem is that our neighbors, even my children's teachers, mistake my children's stepmother for me. It infuriates me. I have even gotten comments like, "Oh you're the brunette." My husband's new wife is blonde."

If you are jealous by nature, joint physical custody may not be for you, because it demands constant communication with your ex-spouse, and if they remarry, with their new spouse. For the good of the whole, you are constantly mediating, asking their opinions, and compromising. If this is difficult for you, don't attempt this solution. Your children will suffer, and you will end up with ulcers.

Suggestions to Help Joint Physical Custody Work

1. *Be assertive.* To eliminate confusion when your children play with friends, make it a point to introduce yourself to parents and explain your living situation. Explain that your children have two homes and they will have to interact with both parents at different times. Stepparents may be involved and parents of friends should also be aware of this.

2. *Rules should be consistent.* The rules at both homes should be the same, for example, curfews, table manners, what TV shows the children may watch, but if they are not, this should be explained to the children openly and not as a put-down or judgment of the other parent. Say something like, "I know you are allowed to watch television at your father's, but here it makes me uncomfortable. I will have to talk to him about that," rather than "Your father is so stupid. How dare he let an eight-year-old watch that smut?"

3. *Alert the school.* Officials at your child's school should know of your living situation because they need contact phone numbers and addresses should an emergency arise. Make it a point to discuss in person your joint physical custody living situation with the school secretary, nurse, and principal. If there is a counselor on campus, she should also understand your child's living situation.

   At the start of the school year, introduce yourself to your child's new teacher. If possible, have all parents from both families meet with the teacher at the same time so that she can attach names to faces. Explain that you need two of everything—two newsletters, two school picture forms, two student-of-the-month awards, two report cards, and two student conferences. Now they know who you are! Another good idea is to supply the teacher with a schedule of when your child is at their father's and when your child is at your house.

4. *Take things in your stride.* You cannot be responsible for other's insensitive remarks. Comments like, "Oh you're the brunette" are meant to push your buttons. They have nothing to do with the fact that you are trying to raise healthy, happy children in the wake of divorce.

"If we share joint physical custody of the children, will child support still be an issue, even if the kids live with each of us 50 percent of the time?"

Child support is not based on the type of custody agreement but on the needs of the children. Parents who are awarded joint physical custody of their children (50/50), pay an amount of child support based on the ratio of each parent's income to their combined incomes, and the amount of time the children spend at each house. More simply, if for example, you make 70 percent of your combined income, you may still pay your ex-spouse child support even though the kids live with you 50 percent of the time.

Joint Custody with Joint Physical Custody Parent Panel

In the following section, parents speak honestly about the joint physical custody solution.

"Why did you choose this custody solution?"

SALLY WILLIAMS: "Even though Charlie and I could not live together, I honestly believed it was in the best interest of my children to see both their mother and their father as often as possible."

CHARLIE FORD: "Am I being honest? There were many things that Sally and I did not agree upon when we were married. Ironically, one of our biggest differences was how we handled the children. Our values were different. I knew we were getting a divorce and I wanted my children to be exposed to my values, as well as Sally's, then make up their mind when they were adults. I have never told my children I do not agree with their mother philosophically, but that was the true reason I wanted to stay in my children's lives. But I have to admit, I had no idea what I was getting myself into when we started this years ago. To say it has taught me patience is an understatement."

"Would you choose this custody solution again?"

SALLY WILLIAMS: "I would, definitely, and that is an unselfish response, because it has not been easy. Three years ago, my husband was transferred to Los Angeles, four hundred miles away from our home. Because we have joint physical custody, if I moved, I would have given up my right to see them. The custody agreement was 50 percent of the time with me and 50 percent of the time with my ex. I was now in the position of having to choose between living with my husband or my children. We have worked out a plan where my husband lives four days a week in Los Angeles and three days a week at home (Livermore, California), but it is by no means something I want to do much longer."

CHARLIE FORD: "What is the alternative? I think if I chose any other custody solution than this one, I would not have been able to see my children as much as I wanted. Being that my children really live with me, not just visit on the weekends, I am the one who cooks dinner and comforts them if they have a nightmare. I probably wouldn't have been the one to do that if I were still married to their mother. In a way, joint physical custody has allowed me to be the father I really wanted to be—even with the divorce."

FRANCES PEARLSTEIN: "I can only make observations because I came into this relationship when I married Louise's ex-husband, Don, but what I see are two very unselfish parents attempting to set the best example possible for their children. Don't get me wrong, they falter, but they try from their heart to resolve conflicts for the sake of the children, not the parents. Louise has gone out of her way to integrate my daughter Haley into the lives of her children. That must not be easy. It has taught me to be a much more unselfish person."

DONALD PEARLSTEIN: "If I had to make the choice, probably, but it can be stressful."

MITCH JEFFERSON: "It did not work for us. I believe the main reason was that Lucy was just too angry at me about the divorce. She couldn't let a lot of things go, which spilled over into our everyday lives. Consistency was a major concern. She used breaking the rules we had agreed upon as a weapon to undermine my authority with the kids, and total chaos broke out."

PAT DENNY: "I would, but I'm the one trying to juggle multiple divorces, so that means I'm willing to tackle just about anything! But nothing has happened while attempting joint physical custody to completely convince me that this was not the right choice for my children."

"How did this custody solution affect the kids?"

LOUISE (PEARLSTEIN) BARTELL: "I think that choosing joint physical custody has taught my children positive tools for resolving conflict. They see their father and me interact on a daily basis and watch us search for ways to resolve conflict without fighting or insulting each other. I hope I am a living demonstration that peace is better than war."

MITCH JEFFERSON: "*Joint physical custody* did not work for us. The kids were sick and I was sick. Lucy was angry all the time. We just couldn't do it. Lucy and I could not stop disagreeing long enough to set the example we knew we needed to in order for our children to be emotionally healthy. Our family's solution needed to be more conventional, where the parents did not interact so frequently. Simply, *joint custody* works well for us. The kids live with Lucy, see me on a regular basis, and we discuss all decisions before they are made."

SALLY WILLIAMS: "If I didn't wholeheartedly believe this was the best solution for my children, I would have fought for another solution. I believe having both my ex-husband and me as an active part of their lives has kept our children grounded after the divorce."

"How did it affect your life after divorce?"

CHARLIE FORD: "I am glad I did it, but it hasn't been easy. Joint physical custody has allowed me to stay active in my children's lives. I know exactly what's going on with them at school and in their personal lives, which I may not have known if I had opted for a more conventional type of custody agreement. However, the things that bothered me before in regards to Sally's parenting style still bother me, but now I just laugh at them. At our parents' discussions I even tease her a little about them, and it has become a sort of family joke . . . mainly because her husband agrees with me, but we don't want to get into that."

SALLY WILLIAMS: "As I mentioned, I couldn't just leave town when my second husband got transferred. I had to make other arrangements, which has been difficult. Basically, I was forced to choose between my husband and my children, a difficult decision I don't wish on anyone."

Please note: There is an epilogue to Sally Williams's story. She recently informed me that after two and a half years of living only three days a week with her second husband, he announced he could no longer live in that manner and filed for a divorce. Remember, the joint physical custody solution affects *everyone* concerned and should be considered very carefully.

PAT DENNY: "It has taught me to be organized, plus the mediation and communication skills I have mastered have helped me in other phases of my life. I wouldn't have dreamed I would ever say this, but if I can get along with my husband's ex-wife, I can get along with anybody."

CHAPTER SIX

Bird's Nest Custody:

A Rare and Exotic Solution

"It is common sense to take a method, try it. If it fails, admit it frankly and try another. But above all, try something."

—FRANKLIN D. ROOSEVELT

"I wanted the divorce," admits Chris Ward, a recently divorced mother of two. "It was a dysfunctional marriage, but the girls were never subjected to what went on . . . the divorce was a great surprise to them and I realized how detrimental it could be if they were to be used as 'trophies.' So I set out to come up with an arrangement that would make the best of a bad situation."

Chris decided to get an apartment around the corner, and her husband kept the house. The girls continued to live in their home. This arrangement allowed them to maintain their original bedrooms, pets, etc. "We decided the girls would stay with their dad each night, and that I would come over each morning, get them up, get them ready, then take them to school, just as I had done all their lives. No waking up early to go to sitters. Basically, nothing changed with their morning routine," she explains. After school, Chris picked up the girls and brought them back to her apartment for after-school snacks, homework, or to "chill together with some Nickelodeon." The girls also stay late a couple nights a week so they can have dinner with their mother. The weekend arrangement is the standard every-other-weekend scenario. "Because we share basically the same amount of time with the girls, we agreed there would be no child support. If the girls need something, we take care of it," she adds.

Another name for Chris's solution is bird's nest custody. Actually, true bird's nest custody is a joint custody arrangement that takes things one step further: Both parents move in and out at different intervals, while the children stay in the home. For this to work, however, the couple must figure out how to maintain a household together for the children and separate households for themselves. You would think an obvious prerequisite would be good communication between the parents, but Chris reports otherwise. "I realize this sort of arrangement would not work for everyone, but I am testimony that even in divorces that aren't so friendly (and ours, while it appeared to be civil on the surface, was full of animosity on the part of my ex because I initiated the separation), if you keep in mind that the children are ultimately the ones who wind up the most hurt and focus on avoiding that at all costs, it indeed can be done."

Chris realizes things may change in the future. She anticipates that a new wife may not like her coming into the home every morning to wake up her children. "But I will still be able to pick them up and take them to school and pick them up in the afternoon. I fully intend to compromise as time moves on. My first priority is my children."

Other Nests

Brian and Jeanne Cromwell have four daughters. They are in the entertainment business and have converted the entire front part of their home, including the garage, into a business office and sound studio. The bedrooms are in the back half of the home. The kitchen lies somewhere in the middle. Although the girls are well on their way to stardom, Brian and Jeanne did not fare as well. They filed for divorce last year, agreeing to joint physical custody.

Because of the girls' hectic travel schedule, Brian and Jeanne decided it would be too chaotic to ask the girls to travel back and forth between each parent's home, so they decided the best solution for them was for the girls to stay in their own rooms, continue to practice and record, and they, the parents, would take turns moving in and out every two weeks. Jeanne bought a home near the beach, Brian has an apartment around the corner from the original family home. "It sounds unconventional," Jeanne says, "but our life has always been unconventional. No one even bats an eye when they hear about our arrangement. I have always wanted to live near the water and when we came up with this idea, that is where I bought my home," she adds. "For us, to buy another home was the solution. We were lucky we could afford it. This type of arrangement is not cheap."

An Uncommon Solution

Terrence is ten and was born with spina bifida. Confined to a wheelchair, his father converted their two-story home, complete with widened hallways, wheelchair ramps, and low-access light switches, so Terrence could feel as self-sufficient as possible while growing up. The conversion was done over a five-year period and was costly. Maya and Leon Smith, Terrence's parents, decided to divorce last year, but it would be far too expensive to replace their Terrence-friendly home. Bird's nest custody was their solution.

Maya and Leon also share an apartment about two miles from

their primary residence. When Maya lives with Terrence, Leon lives in the apartment. When Leon lives with Terrence, Maya lives in the apartment. "I am not naive. I know we can only do this for a little while," Maya laughs, "at least until one of us meets someone else. I can't imagine someone moving in and out with me every other week, but we have been doing this for a year. It was the least disruptive solution for Terrence. So far, so good."

It is obvious that this custody solution does not work for everyone, but because of their special circumstances, bird's nest custody was the solution these families thought worked best for them.

"I Didn't Know What Else to Do."

Or so said Sophia Lopez when asked why she and her husband, Gerald, decided upon a bird's nest custody arrangement. Sophia's guilt was so profound after her six-year marriage ended because of her affair with a co-worker, she proposed a bird's nest custody solution. She did not want to disrupt her children, and from our interview, she was extremely remorseful about the pain she had caused Gerald.

After months of consideration, this is what Sophia proposed and Gerald agreed to. Sophia's parents had recently passed away and left her their home in their will. Sophia was vice president of marketing for a large corporation, traveled often, and brought home a six-figure salary. Since she made more money than Gerald and inherited a home close by, she offered to buy her husband a condominium as part of the divorce decree. The children would stay in their original home with one of the parents for a month at a time. Gerald would retire to his condo on his off months; Sophia would live in the home she inherited.

"I found out about Sophia's affair with a co-worker completely by accident. It is an understatement to say I was not happy with Sophia, but I was even more upset by how she disrupted our children's lives. By the time we went to court, I would have agreed to anything that would have minimized the pain my children would suffer. Not moving them from their room and the house they knew all their lives seemed like a good solution for now. I wasn't looking to the future."

And the solution evidently worked for two years, until Gerald became serious with another woman who was not interested in moving back and forth every other month. Ironically, Sophia's affair ended soon after Gerald found out.

In every case interviewed, bird's nest custody was only a temporary custody solution. It was feasible when there was no other spouse introduced into the relationship. As soon as someone else became part of the scenario or one of the original parents committed to another relationship or remarried, the families switched to a more conventional custody agreement.

"Is bird's nest custody legal in every state?"

It is a form of joint custody. While joint custody is legal in every state, bird's nest custody may not be as readily accepted in one state as in another. As in all custody cases, the final say is always with the court.

"How do you work out the logistics in bird's nest custody? For example, are the homes or apartments retained in both spouses names?"

Each case is different. The property settlement is handled the same as in any divorce. It is up to the divorcing individuals.

Bird's Nest Custody Parent Panel

In this section, parents answer personal questions about choosing the bird's nest custody solution after their divorce.

"Would you choose this custody solution again?"

CHRIS WARD: "I realize this is pretty unorthodox, and I don't know anyone in this area, or anywhere for that matter, who has come up with something like this. However, I feel it has made a big difference in [the lives of] my children and their adjustment to the new situation. I know many children whose parents' divorces completely altered every aspect of their lives, and that was what I wanted to avoid more than anything. It is an alternative I feel more divorced couples should consider."

MAYA SMITH: "Under the circumstances, this was as close as we could come to staying together for the sake of the children."

"What would you change?"

JEANNE CROMWELL: "Believe it or not, my life is not that much different from when Brian and I were married. We parented together, but one of us was always on the road with the girls. So, I would change nothing. But I may feel differently if I want to remarry. I can't imagine this custody solution would work if either Brian or I remarried."

"How has this custody solution affected your children?"

CHRIS WARD: "I am encouraged often by teachers and friends who comment on how well the girls seem to be doing. We have suffered no behavioral symptoms or signs of distress. All three have continued to be excellent students and are involved in many activities in school and church, etc.

"I think if more people acted like the adults in the divorce situation, we would see fewer children completely devastated by the divorce, and children who are more capable of dealing with a situation that admittedly is difficult to understand."

LEON SMITH: "Terrence has always been an unconventional child. He was not supposed to live past two years old, so every day I have with him I regard as a blessing. Maya and I both agreed that it was our obligation to him to make his life as comfortable as possible, and that is what we are trying to do.

"He does not appear to have any emotional problems brought on by our divorce, but he is very 'to himself,' so it would be difficult to tell. We have him in counseling, and all reports are stable."

Custody Solutions for Same-Sex Parents and Parents of Children Born Outside of Marriage

"Beware lest you lose the substance by grasping at the shadow."

—AESOP

Considering the increased divorce rate, a greater acceptance of a single woman's right to choose, and the gay and lesbian lifestyle, custody of children raised by a single parent or in a same-sex relationship is now a concern of many people. But current custody laws do not serve such a diverse group. While the laws are easily understood for single parents or heterosexual couples, special attention should be given to custody laws that apply directly to the homosexual community.

The Gay and Lesbian Dilemma

"Gay and lesbian partners currently find themselves in a perplexing situation," says Sally Elkington, an attorney from Oakland,

California, who specializes in gay and lesbian issues. "They are asking a court to make decisions for them in custody cases when there are no laws on the books that pertain to their lifestyle, so the judge must make a custody ruling based on the law for married heterosexual couples."

There is a problem with this reasoning. When considering custody of a child produced by a heterosexual couple, married or not, it is likely that the parents are biologically related to the child. This is not true when considering custody of a child raised by a same-sex couple. More often than not, the child in question is physically related to only one of the parents, and when this is the case, if nothing is previously stipulated by the courts, the parent that is not biologically related to the child has very few rights.

"Must a couple be legally married to have questions concerning the custody of their children if they separate?"

No. Therefore, when any two people—gay or straight—who have legal guardianship of a child, divorce or sever the relationship, a question as to who has custody of that child arises.

Background Regarding Same-Sex Marriage

"Is same-sex marriage legal in any state?"

There is currently no state that offers the same legal recognition or respect to same-sex coupling as to heterosexual marriage, but this does not stop people from proclaiming they are married to each other and raising children within that environment. Hawaii, Alaska, and Vermont all have court cases pending to decide if same-sex marriages are legal. Nonetheless, it appears it is less likely that gay and lesbian marriages will be recognized.

Many believed Hawaii would be the first state to recognize

same-sex marriages and give same-sex partners status equal to heterosexual marriage in the eyes of the law because cases questioning the constitutionality of denying marriage licenses to same-sex couples have been before the courts since 1991. Then in 1996, a trial court in Hawaii ruled that the state's ban on same-sex marriages violates the equal protection clause of the Hawaiian Constitution. The court ruling, a landmark case, held that Hawaii had failed to meet its burden under the Hawaiian Supreme Court decision to offer a "compelling" reason to maintain a discriminatory practice. It was found that the state "failed to present sufficient credible evidence . . . that the public interest in the well-being of children and families, or the optimal development of children would be adversely affected by same-sex marriages."

As a result, state lawmakers then agreed to let the voters decide on "Question 2," a constitutional amendment that would expand the power of state lawmakers to restrict marriages to opposite-sex couples. To the surprise of many, the amendment passed in November of 1998, making same-sex marriage illegal in the state of Hawaii.

Alaska has a similar history to Hawaii in regard to recognizing same-sex marriage. A superior court judge recently refused to throw out a challenge to a 1996 law that banned same-sex marriage based on the fact that the judge felt choosing a life partner is a fundamental law protected by the Alaskan Constitution, but "Measure 2," an initiative to amend the state constitution, was approved by the voters 68–32 percent, and as in Hawaii, voters in the 1998 Alaskan election felt that the institution of marriage should be limited only to couples of the opposite sex.

As of this writing, twenty-nine states have bans blocking same-sex marriage. But, the legality of same-sex marriage is not really the issue. Most gay or lesbian parents know there are no formal laws on the books recognizing their union and protecting their custodial rights, and for this reason children raised in a same-sex relationship are most likely the biological or adopted children of only one of the participating partners. With this arrangement, when a gay or lesbian couple separate, the child usually goes with the legal parent. Raising a child as your own and then losing the right to see them if you separate from their biological parent is an extremely emotional issue for the gay and lesbian community—a good reason why we may see more same-sex custody cases before the courts in the near future.

"Is same-sex marriage recognized anywhere?"

There are very few places in the world where gay and lesbian relationships are legally recognized. In Denmark and Norway, a gay or lesbian couple may file a registered partnership, which grants the partners full inheritance rights and the same spousal support responsibilities as a married heterosexual couple. If the relationship ends, they are legally required to file for divorce. Sweden allows same-sex partners the same common law rights as any unmarried couple, and there is a domestic partners law recognized by the French.

"In this day and age, is it still possible that a parent could lose custody of their child if they are gay or lesbian?"

In a case when only one parent is gay and the other continues to be heterosexual after divorce, that knowledge may signal a court to greatly restrict the gay parent's visitation or perhaps even deny custody. There are a few states where a parent's sexual preference cannot interfere with a parent's right to custody of their child, but this still may not guarantee a gay or lesbian parent custody. The final decision always lies with the court, and if you find a judge with an inherent adversity to gays or lesbians, a gay or lesbian parent may very well lose custody of their child.

"For the sake of comparison, is it possible for a single woman to lose custody of her child because she never married the acknowledged father?"

The final decision in a custody dispute is at the mercy of a judge, who in his sincere endeavor to remain impartial, is still only human.

Custody Problems Specific to the Homosexual Community

Traditional mother and father roles are ingrained in us by society. Even though men now accept more of the nurturing role and women spend more time in the workplace, if you ask the average person who the primary nurturing parent is in their family, the most frequent response is the mother. But in a same-sex relationship, a "mother" may not exist. And to further confront conventional thinking, the participating same-sex partners may decide that the biological parent should not be the primary caregiver of the child in question. Instead, the other partner should take on the primary nurturing responsibilities. In such cases, when a gay or lesbian couple separates, a parent who has taken care of a child all their life may have no legal recourse to see that child after separation.

"Custody problems? I'll give you custody problems," says Tracy, a thirty-two-year-old lesbian. Her partner of the last three years, Eleanor, had two sons when they met. This fulfilled Tracy's lifelong desire to have children but also caused huge problems when, three months ago, Eleanor and Tracy ended their relationship.

"The boys were my children," explains Tracy. "I was the one who drove them to basketball games, made their lunches, and helped them with their homework. Now I have no legal right to see them. Because I love them so much, I tried to keep my presence consistent even after their mother and I split, but this was causing a lot of friction, which was obvious to the boys."

Tracy felt she was being denied a right she was once granted by being in a live-in relationship with the boys' mother. This hurt her and she felt also hurt the boys, a position with which many divorcing stepparents can sympathize. However, in court, a heterosexual stepparent's requests for visitation of their ex-spouse's children may be given more credence simply because their marriage to the children's biological mother or father was legally recognized. Plus, a judge's own prejudice against homosexuals can come into play.

"When we were together, the agreement to help raise the boys was a verbal one made between Eleanor and me. We asked Eleanor's ex-husband if he would consent to some sort of agreement being drawn up, but he said absolutely not. Because he and Eleanor have joint custody and he objected to any agreement confirming my future interaction with the boys, none was ever made. Now that we have split up, visitation schedules must be agreed upon by Eleanor and me, and although I get along well with the boys' biological father, if he says I may not continue my relationship with the boys, I have no legal recourse."

Surrogate Motherhood or Artificial Insemination

Another custody problem increasing within the gay community is when a surrogate mother or artificial insemination is used to produce a child. In these cases, the other partner, the one who did not contribute biologically to creating the child, must legally adopt the child should they want to ensure visitation upon the couple's separation. This is termed a *second-parent adoption* and sounds easier than it really is. Since many states make it difficult for same-sex relationships to thrive, and even pass laws to discourage homosexual partnering, a second-parent adoption procedure may take far longer than necessary.

"What is the difference between a second-parent adoption, a de facto adoption, and a limited-consent adoption?"

Technically, they are all the same type of adoption. In the past, when someone who is *not married* to the biological parent was allowed to adopt that biological parent's child, it was referred to as a de facto adoption. To make the language friendlier, this type of adoption was then called a second-parent adoption. The procedure is now called a limited-consent adoption, because in essence that is what it is. The biological parent retains their right as a parent but also allows another person to adopt their child. This type of adoption is used when a child is born to a homosexual or lesbian, who wishes their life partner to also adopt their child. If the child is adopted, both parents, same-sex or not, have the right to sue for custody should they terminate their relationship.

"What is the difference between a two-parent adoption and a second-parent adoption?"

A second-parent adoption is an adoption granted to the unmarried partner of the biological parent. A two-parent adoption is an adoption of a child granted to two unmarried people.

"If a second-parent adoption would guarantee both partners in a same-sex relationship the right to possible custody of their child after separation, why doesn't everyone do it?"

"Money," explains attorney Elkington. Each state charges a state adoption fee. In the state of California, it's about $1,500. That alone may prevent gay and lesbian couples from starting the procedure. Then there are attorney fees, and some couples just don't have that sort of extra cash."

There are other reasons a couple may not seek a second-parent adoption, for example, legal entanglements. One of the partners may still be legally married to someone else, plus there is a wealth of misinformation that confuses prospective couples.

"I would do it," says Michelle, a working mother in her thirties, who just had a child by artificial insemination. "But in our research, we found I would have to give up my rights as a mother to allow [her partner] Janine to adopt the baby."

"That, of course, is untrue," replies Elkington. "But it's the kind of misinformation that's out there. A second-parent adoption, better called a limited-consent adoption, does not require you to terminate your own rights. It grants rights to another person while retaining your rights to parent." No one may have explained to Michelle the laws concerning a conventional adoption. For example, an unwed teenage mother has a child and decides to give up that child for adoption. Under those circumstances, the mother is relinquishing all future rights to the child. But Michelle's case is different. She had the child, acknowledged it is hers, and wants to raise it, granting joint custody to a life partner.

Specific things need to be done to guarantee that a second-parent adoption is done correctly. "There are no laws that specifically state same-sex partners cannot adopt children," explains Elkington. "When there is no legislation to support what you are doing, sometimes you have to come round from the back door. For example, no forms are specifically written for gay and lesbian parents to adopt children. We must use conventional adoption forms designed for married heterosexual couples, but we make the necessary legal maneuvers to get the job done."

The final goal in filing for a limited-consent adoption is to protect your partner, your child, and you from unnecessary pain if a separation does occur. An attorney well versed in limited-consent adoption could advise you.

Another, more personal reason a gay or lesbian couple may not opt for a second-parent adoption is fear of future discrimination for their children. If names of people of the same gender appear on a birth certificate, it is obvious that the child was raised by gay or lesbian parents. "In a world where there is strong discrimination of homosexuals and lesbians, some of my clients fear their children will also be put in that position should various decision makers, future employers, for example, find that they were raised by gay or lesbian parents. Basically," Elkington concludes, "with a second-parent adoption in place, gay and lesbian parents have the right to fight for custody should they separate, just like everyone else. It's not a win/win situation, is it?"

Gay and Lesbian Stepparenting—Not So Different

Let's examine additional questions that may be raised by same-sex couples, as well as look at solutions offered by people who have had these experiences.

"What do therapists say about the basic development of children brought up in same-sex relationships?"

Studies show that child development is the same in loving, same-sex relationships as it is in heterosexual relationships. However, the child-development aspect of being raised by a same-sex couple was not what concerned many therapists interviewed on the subject. From a clinical standpoint, all agreed that love and stability were the main considerations to the positive development of a child. But, as Cindy Blackett, a licensed family and child counselor who has treated gay patients, explains, "Studies show that kids' development is the same if the environment is a positive one. As children raised in a same-sex relationship move into adolescence and the teenage years, their friends often tease them. That's when having same-sex parents may be painful for a child: when dealing with the teasing."

In these circumstances, therapy can be helpful for both parent and child. First, the parent can prepare the child for teasing and reinforce positive self-esteem. Second, for the child, if teasing does begin, therapy is an excellent forum to allow a child to talk about their feelings and learn constructive rather than destructive ways to cope with their life situation.

"I have heard the term co-parent used in regard to parenting in the gay and lesbian community. What is the difference between a co-parent and a stepparent?"

Any stepparent is a co-parent, but a co-parent does not have to be a stepparent. Confusing? A stepparent is the person who has married someone who already has children and assumes the role of parent when the children are in their presence. The key word is *married*. Since gay and lesbian couples are unable to legally marry, they cannot legally be stepparents. Call them what you will, in this instance, stepparents and co-parents fulfill the same role.

"What rights does the gay partner leaving a relationship have in regards to visitation after separation if the child in question is the biological offspring of their ex-partner and the other biological parent still claims rights to that child?"

If the other biological parent is living and participating in the child's life, there is not much a gay or lesbian ex-partner can do to ensure visitation after separation. Technically, the legal questions of custody and visitation have already been answered when the biological parents were divorced or when legal guardianship was established by the biological or legally adoptive parents.

Tracy's Dilemma—Not That Uncommon

Tracy faced the same problem many heterosexual stepparents face when they grow close to their stepchildren and then divorce the children's biological parent. My own stepchildren are sixteen and thirteen and are now old enough to continue a relationship with me on their own should something happen to our only legal link—their father. But when they were small, I will admit to sleepless nights contemplating how often I would be allowed to see them should their father pass on unexpectedly.

My husband and his ex-wife have joint custody and joint physical custody of their children. As you know from reading chapter five, "Joint Custody with Joint Physical Custody," this means the children live with each parent 50 percent of the time. In my case, my stepchildren live with my husband and me for the first two weeks of the month, and with their biological mother the last two weeks of the month. I have helped raise them and when asked how many children I have, I have never distinguished between my biological or stepchildren. My answer has always been, "I have four children."

When I expressed my concerns to my husband, he said, "Why wouldn't it just stay the way it is?" He took it for granted that if he passed on, the children would continue to go back and forth, just as they always had. I had to explain that custody was not like property. I didn't inherit the custody rights to his children because I was his wife. There was nothing that legally guaranteed I could continue my relationship with his kids. My husband ended the conversation with, "Don't worry. Nothing will happen." And, thank God, it has not, but like everyone else in this position, I share the same concern: If, for some reason, something happened, I might lose my right to participate in my stepchildren's lives.

"That isn't exactly true," explains Elkington. "You would have a little better chance to sue for visitation because you were legally married to their father. There are laws that support you, because heterosexual marriage is legally recognized. But the biological mother would probably prevail, just as the biological parent would prevail in a gay or lesbian lawsuit."

Tracy explains her plight. "I knew when I was leaving the boys' mother that I was getting a divorce of sorts, but I had no idea it meant I had to leave the boys, too. I don't know what I was thinking, but I believed things would almost remain the same. I didn't give up the condo I owned, even though I had established residence with the boys' mother for three years. When we split up, I just moved back into my condo down the street. Every morning I saw the boys leave for school and worried if they had remembered to make a lunch. I still went to their basketball games to cheer them on. In a heterosexual divorce, the pain is well-known, but when a gay relationship ends, you have no idea of the pain of separation when you have no claim on the children you love as your own, especially since I will probably never have any of my own."

Tracy wanted to continue her relationship with Eleanor's boys but could do nothing if Eleanor denied her permission. Custody was already established when the biological parents divorced. No agreement was drawn between Tracy and Eleanor when they lived together, and even if they had attempted to put something on paper, it would not have stood up in court. Eleanor and her ex-husband held joint custody. Tracy had no legal recourse. "It wasn't because my ex-wife chose a lesbian lifestyle," explains Doug, Eleanor's ex-husband. "I have to admit, it was a shock at first, but it wasn't Tracy's gender that prevented me from agreeing to a legal document. I would have made the same protest should my ex-wife have remarried a man and asked for the same guarantee, that if they divorce, her ex-husband would have legal visitation rights to my children. I would never give up my rights to my kids."

The ending of a relationship may sever the parents'/step-parents' ties to each other but not their emotional ties to the children. When their same-sex relationship ended, Tracy wanted visitation rights but had no recourse. "My main concern was consistency for the boys. We had gone through a lot over the years. We had dealt with the fact we lived as a lesbian couple in a very small town. I was accepted as one of the boys' caregivers. They had grown accustomed to my presence. They knew I loved them, and they loved me. They had already gone through one divorce when their mother and father separated. I didn't want the pain of our separation to upset them any more than it had to."

Psychological or Equitable Parent

If Eleanor had sole custody of her boys, or their biological father had died before she met Tracy, Tracy may have had a chance of gaining visitation by appealing to a court to be proclaimed an equitable or psychological parent. (The difference is explained in chapter two.) However, Kate Kendell, the executive director of the National Center for Lesbian Rights, and an attorney specializing in family law and gay and lesbian civil rights, says this may only be an option in states sensitive to the plight of same-sex partners. Some states, namely, South Dakota, Texas, Utah, Georgia, and now Hawaii and Alaska, have recently passed legislation to hinder same-sex marriages. "In the ten years we have litigated cases of this sort, we have positive decisions as often a negative. I can think of six cases in the last ten years where a past partner was legally proclaimed a psychological parent."

When asked if there were any states that were particularly sensitive to the plight of same-sex parents, she says, "The decision is purely at the discretion of the court."

Although attitudes toward same-sex relationships have relaxed, gay or lesbian partners and heterosexual stepparents may be better advised to try to stay on speaking terms with their ex-partners and appeal to everyone's good nature in order to continue a relationship with the children.

As suggested, the solution to Tracy's problem was not found through her ex-partner, the children's mother, but through their biological father. He and Tracy had established a friendship and mutual respect over the years and he did not share his ex-wife's anger regarding their breakup. Tracy found it much easier to work out a visitation schedule with the boys' father. "In the beginning, it was just easier to deal with Mark. When he had the kids, I occasionally went over for dinner. When he needed help picking up the boys, he often called me. As time went on, Mark remarried and his new wife took on the responsibilities to which I had grown accustomed, but the ability to talk to Mark rationally and work out a visitation schedule made the initial separation from the boys a lot easier to take."

"If a gay or lesbian parent has allowed their partner to adopt their biological child and then they separate, may the adoptive parent sue for custody?"

If the parent has adopted the child, they have all the legal rights of an adoptive parent, which means they would be allowed to sue for custody should the couple "divorce," and if that was not granted, they would be entitled to visitation. Because adoptive parents are just as legally responsible for their children as biological parents, they may also be required to pay child support.

Which brings to mind the case of Pam Lockrem-West of Sacramento, California, and her former partner. Pam and her partner planned to have two children. The first child would be conceived using a sperm donor, and so the children would be biologically related, the couple planned to use the same donor to have the second child. The two women agreed the ex would be the first to conceive, and Pam would then adopt the child through a second-parent adoption. She would pay all the expenses for the artificial insemination, prenatal care, and delivery, then become pregnant herself, and her ex was to accept the financial responsibility of that pregnancy and delivery. It was agreed when that child was born, her ex would adopt that baby as Pam had adopted the first child. Both she and her ex hyphenated their last names, which the children would take as their own.

The plan soured when it took a little longer than expected to finalize the first second-parent adoption. By the time the firstborn child was two and a half years old, the adoption had still not been finalized. Pam and her ex began to have problems. Even though the couple tried counseling, the ex wanted to leave the relationship. Because she was the child's biological mother, she took the baby and moved out. Six months later, Pam received a letter from her ex-partner, stating she wanted only one mother for her daughter and all contact was to be discontinued.

In Pam's mind, her child had been taken from her. She petitioned family court for temporary visitation, which was granted, but her ex immediately appealed the decision. She and her ex were ordered into mediation, but the ex did not comply. She simply did not show up. What recourse does Pam have?

"Not much," says Kendell. "This case came before the courts in the state of California. You would think that because of the high population of gay and lesbian couples there the courts would be sensitive to Pam's dilemma. But the laws are archaic, to say the least."

These "archaic" laws prompted Pam to take another approach. She sued her ex-partner in civil court for breach of contract, but after another lengthy battle, she lost again.

This situation inspired Pam Lockrem-West and her new partner, Dania Lukey, to found My Other Mother, or MOM, which is dedicated to helping gay and lesbian parents gain visitation rights after separation. The Sacramento-based group's lack of funding has prevented it from really getting off the ground.

"Of course, the idea for the organization grew from the problems Pam had when trying to visit her own daughter," says Lukey. "Our desire is to call attention to this kind of situation. Most lawyers we talked to told Pam she had no rights as a parent."

"Many of these problems would be eliminated," suggests Kendell, "if there was specific legislation that pertained to gay and lesbian couples. We are working with laws written for heterosexual couples, which really don't pertain to us. All gay and lesbian couples want right now is the ability to be heard in court and petition for visitation. We will start there."

"Our main thrust will be to hold fund-raisers and place ads in magazines that are normally channeled to straight parents but are increasingly read by gay and lesbian parents looking for advice. By raising awareness of the issue, we hope to let other gay parents realize they are not alone."

Michael and Scott

Whether you approve of homosexuality or not, the quandary gay and lesbian parents face continues. In the case of Michael and Scott, two gay men raising Scott's biological daughter, Krista, conceived with the help of a surrogate mother, religious affiliations kept Scott's sister, Mary Louise, from accepting her brother's homosexuality wholeheartedly. While she tolerated her brother's lifestyle and shared a warm relationship with Scott's daughter and partner, in theory, she did not believe two gay men should raise a daughter.

Michael and Scott had lived together for eight years and the decision to raise a child together was a mutual one. They did not care if the child was a boy or a girl, they just wanted the child to be biologically related to one of them.

Together Michael and Scott searched for a surrogate mother. Scott designed extensive interview questions, and they agreed upon the woman who would act as a surrogate mother. The child was conceived through artificial insemination. Nine months later, Krista was born.

Because of Scott's obvious dedication to the relationship, Michael never felt it necessary to formally adopt Krista. In an effort to be part of the birthing process, Michael even co-signed all the release papers from the hospital. But release papers are not legal birth records, and when Scott unexpectedly died in a car accident, his sister petitioned the court for legal custody of the child. Scott's sister won, and Michael was no longer granted visitation. Krista was nine years old at the time of the decision.

"How long does a second-parent (limited-consent) adoption usually take?"

A second-parent adoption usually takes about six months to finalize.

"Is there any other precaution a gay or lesbian couple can take to prevent custody problems should their same-sex relationship end?"

A second-parent or limited-consent adoption guarantees your ability to fight for your custodial rights in court. If you don't qualify for a second-parent adoption, it is a good idea for gay and lesbian couples that plan to raise children together to formalize this decision by writing a Parenting Plan, the same type of agreement, suggested in chapter two, when a heterosexual couple divorces. The difference in these two agreements is the approach. After the relationship ends, the Parenting Plan is drawn up to establish your responsibilities when parenting together after divorce. A Parenting Plan written by a gay or lesbian couple, in essence, does the same thing but is written at the beginning of the relationship in order to establish joint custody in the minds of the participating parents. Kendell of the National Center for Lesbian Rights' explains, "Although not a legal document per se, as more and more of these cases are heard by the courts, having a Parenting Plan that clearly states the responsibilities of the two parents involved is critical to favorably settling a custody case."

The Center suggests the following points be included in a Parenting Plan when a gay or lesbian couple is contemplating raising a child together. (Please note, this is only a suggestion, and additional points specific to your relationship may need to be added.)

- the name and birth date of the child
- a statement indicating that conception or adoption was a joint decision
- an agreement to share equally in child-rearing roles stating the following:
  - each parent will have joint custody of the child, and all major decisions for the child will be made jointly
  - each child will spend approximately half of his/her time with each parent
  - each parent agrees to pay half the day-to-day living expenses while the parents live together
  - each parent will pay half the costs to provide child care,

religious education, medical and dental care, counseling, or psychotherapy

- each parent will claim the child/children as his/her dependent for tax purposes
- each parent shall maintain a life-insurance policy during his/her minority

- a statement of intent of both parties to continue to provide for the child if the adult relationship dissolves
- a statement indicating that the nonbiological or nonadoptive parent will be guardian of the child in case of incapacitation or death of the biological or adoptive parent
- an agreement to use alternative dispute resolution if a dispute arises
- an acknowledgment that the agreement involves questions not yet settled by statute or the courts
- the terms of visitation, custody, and support if the adult relationship dissolves
- a statement identifying the nonbiological or a nonadoptive parent as a psychological parent
- an acknowledgment that the agreement was signed voluntarily

Attorneys familiar with custody cases brought to court by gay and lesbian parents suggest you cover all your bases. Besides a Parenting Plan, it is also advisable for couples to stipulate in a will their desires for their children in case of death or separation. A Nomination of Guardianship drawn up by an attorney, which explains that you would like your child to reside with your life partner if you die or become incapacitated, is also a good idea. "None of these documents guarantee anything in court," explains Sally Elkington, who also happens to be the former executive director of the National Center for Lesbian Rights and still sits on its board of directors, "but by having all this information down on paper, the judge cannot make a ruling based on the fact that he/she was not certain of the parent's intent." Elkington then adds, "All these questions would be eliminated if gay and lesbian couples were permitted to marry. Because they can't, the simple things a heterosexual couple takes for granted are not available to a gay or lesbian couple. Even after living together for twenty years, a gay or lesbian couple cannot file a joint tax return or automatically inherit property, and of course, child custody is a big question."

Custody Problems Specific to Children Born Outside of Marriage

Much of what has already been discussed in this chapter regarding custody and the same-sex relationship also pertains to the heterosexual single parent who chooses to have a child outside of marriage, because in the eyes of the law, both are single parents.

The main questions concerning custody and the children born outside marriage are:

- How much interaction does the other biological parent really want?
- Is the other biological parent willing to contribute financially to raising the child?

The answers to both questions depend on the individual's situation. If the other biological parent (father) wants to interact with their child, then it is the obligation of the original biological parent (mother) to allow them to do so.

"But I never had anything to do with my child's father," explains Charlotte Greenfield, a single mother from Raleigh, North

Carolina. "All I got when my son was born was a phone call from his father acknowledging the birth and more hogwash about how he couldn't possibly be the father, but by that time I was grateful he was gone, and I wanted a guarantee I would never have to deal with him again. His name doesn't even appear on my son's birth certificate."

This doesn't necessarily happen only to mothers. Duane Gabriels, a twenty-one-year-old single father, also from North Carolina, had a similar problem. "My ex-girlfriend lost interest in our son shortly after he was born. She would take him to concerts and let people she didn't know hold him while she danced the night away. One night a mutual friend picked her up drunk, hitch-hiking at three in the morning. She had our son with her and he hadn't been changed in a long time. The next day she left Davey on my front porch and I never saw her again. It's been two years."

In each case, only one biological parent wished to be respon-sible for their child and wanted to terminate the parental rights of the other to ensure that the lives of their children would not be disrupted in the future. But a parent must be careful. The attempt to terminate the rights of an uninvolved parent may be miscon-strued by the court as an angry and spiteful move not made in the best interest of the child.

Proof is needed to justify something as extreme as the termi-nation of someone's parental rights, for example, as in Charlotte Greenfield's case, no father's name on the birth certificate, no interaction with the child, and no child support paid. Or in Duane Garbriel's situation, there was a history of neglect, and his ex-girlfriend has not seen their child in over two years. Be fore-warned, none of these examples *guarantee* the termination of parental right. They are merely a starting point.

Torrance Harman, an attorney and mediator in Virginia tells us, "The termination of parental rights is viewed seriously by the courts. There are people who have committed terrible crimes and are now in prison, but their parental rights have not been taken from them. It's not an easy thing to do, to remove someone's parental rights, and the laws differ from state to state. I can think of a case in Virginia where both the mother and the father agreed that the parental rights of one parent should end, but the Guardian *ad litem*, or attorney for the child, did not agree and the rights of the parent in question were not terminated."

If you petition the court and the rights of a parent are terminated, child support is no longer an issue. You will no longer be required to pay child support, nor will you be entitled to receive it.

"Is there a question of custody when a woman becomes pregnant and simply decides to keep her child?"

Yes. If the father is known and wants to participate in the child's life, then he may also petition the court for custody after the child is born. If the unmarried father does not receive custody, he is still obliged to financially support the child.

If there is no acknowledged father, the mother is regarded as the child's sole custodial parent.

A special note to unmarried fathers seeking custody of their children: A judge looks carefully at the actions of the unmarried father who seeks custody of his children. If an unmarried father is determined to fight for custody, it is recommended that he demonstrate his intent to the court as soon as possible. Don't wait two years down the road, become angry at the child's mother, and then petition for custody. It is unlikely a judge will take your petition seriously. However, if you show your honorable intent from the beginning, perhaps even when the mother is pregnant, you are more likely to receive positive consideration from a judge.

"I was never married to my son's father and I have legal custody of our son. Can I ever prevent my son's father from seeing our son?"

The only time a biological parent can legally prevent the other acknowledged biological parent from seeing their child is if the child's safety is in question. If abuse is suspected, the other biological parent can then be prosecuted. If abuse is proven, after the offending biological parent has served his sentence, a restraining order may be filed, making it illegal for him to come into contact with the child.

"If I have allowed my child to be adopted, do I have any legal responsibility toward that child, for example, child support?"

If you have allowed your child to be legally adopted by another adult, you have no legal responsibilities for that child.

"I am a single mother who has lived with a man for ten years without the benefit of marriage. We are separating, and he says he will fight for custody of our son. Is this possible?"

A couple does not have to be married to have a custody dispute. If a child has been produced by a union, whether or not they are married, then custody of the child is in question when the union is severed. If both the biological mother and father prove to be fit parents, they will most likely be awarded joint custody.

If an ex-partner is not the biological father of a child when custody is sought, then the ex-partner would be suing for custody based on a psychological connection similar to gay and lesbian couples in this same position. Although some exes have been awarded visitation based on the psychological-parent premise, receiving sole custody based on this connection is far more difficult. This is where a Parenting Plan would have been helpful, so if a lawsuit were brought before the court, a judge could consider the original intent of the biological parent.

"I am a single mother who never married my daughter's father. Although he occasionally pays child support and visits her, payments and visits are sporadic, and I fear this kind of interaction is detrimental to my child's self-esteem. Is there anything I can do?"

If a child feels he/she cannot count on either parent, it is detrimental to their self-esteem. The child perceives the reason the other parent is not visiting them as a personal deficiency. We see this in the response of a six-year-old boy I had the privilege of teaching some years back. For three days, he came to school and told me his father was going to see him on the weekend. With each day his excitement grew. "How many days is it until Friday?" he would ask. I would answer with the appropriate three, then two, then one.

On the following Monday, when the child returned to school, I anxiously asked him how the weekend went with his father. His eyes began to water. His father had forgotten.

Of course, his mother was furious and her apparent anger only served to reinforce the child's insecurity. As a former teacher who has observed these kinds of problems, I tell you that it took a while for this little boy to resume his normal behavior. He was depressed, he would lash out at the other children for what appeared to be no reason, his attention span was short, and he could not keep his mind on his work. At recess, he would not leave my side. I could only be as loving as possible and called a school counselor in for support. This could not prevent his father from repeating the behavior. At one point, I had the opportunity to meet the biological father and I explained his son's reaction to

his inconsistency in visitation. He told me that I had to understand, he "was never married to the child's mother and [he] had
real children at home."

Even as I write this story, I become angry at that father's igno-
rance of his emotional responsibility to his son. I could tell by his
attitude that, in his mind, he thought he was being a pretty good
guy for occasionally showing up in the kid's life, when he had
"real" kids at home. His comment was fleeting, and I did not have
time to tell him that support is more than money. Your child's
ability to depend and look up to you is not predicated on whether
you were ever married to your child's biological parent. Never
marrying your child's biological parent does not eliminate your
obligation to supply both financial and emotional support to your
child.

Sally Elkington's no-nonsense conclusion is spoken from the
heart: "If we, as people, honor the original agreements we make
with each other rather than break them when we are angry and
divorcing, fewer couples—homosexual and heterosexual—would
be fighting custody battles in court. A judge never knows your
child as well as you do."

CHAPTER EIGHT

Child Support:
Payment, Collection, and Modification

"Responsibiilty is the thing people dread most of all. Yet it is the one thing in the world that develops us, gives us manhood or womanhood fibre."

—FRANK CRANE

Child support—perhaps the biggest snarl in the divorce and custody process. Parents hate to pay it, and just as many parents who receive it feel they never get enough to cover their child's expenses. And since financial problems are some of the most difficult to overcome during a marriage, writing a child support check every month may simply open old wounds. But child support is a necessity and a real part of your responsibility to your children after divorce.

Each state requires the parents of a child to pay child support after a divorce, but laws concerning child support and related issues are not consistent from state to state. Legislation is attempting to change this by enlisting federal guidelines to make sure states cooperate with each other when trying to locate deadbeat parents, but child support enforcement is still far from perfect. Parents cannot depend on a judge in one state to support a finding in another state. So know your rights and become familiar with the child support laws in the state where you live.

"Am I entitled to child support?"

If you are the custodial parent, you may be entitled to child support paid by the noncustodial parent. That is, if the custodial parent, in most cases the mother, makes less money than the noncustodial parent, in most cases the father, the custodial parent may receive child support from the noncustodial parent to help raise the child. The reverse also holds true if the father is the custodial parent and he makes less money than the mother. Then she must pay child support. The court also takes into consideration the family's standard of living before the divorce and attempts to keep the children living in the style to which they are accustomed. However, everyone feels the pinch after a divorce. The money that supported one household must now support two.

"For how long am I required to pay child support?"

Child support is to be paid to the custodial parent until the child reaches the age of majority and sometimes longer if they are a college student or disabled. A parent's child support obligations end before the age of majority when the child enters the military service, is emancipated by the court, or if the parent's rights and obligations are terminated because they have allowed their child to be adopted by another party.

"What if we were never married? Do I still have to pay child support?"

This question is most likely asked when a mother has chosen to have a child outside of marriage and is looking for support from the child's father. Support is not based on whether you were married. It is based on the needs of the child. If you are the acknowledged father, whether or not you married the child's mother, you are required to support that child.

"On what do the courts base the amount of child support?"

The amount of child support paid to the custodial parent is determined by the actual needs of the children and the obligated parent's ability to pay, which is generally the amount of money left after bills and taxes. In some states, recreation or automatic deductions for savings accounts or credit unions are ignored by the courts, which feel that child support comes first. Therefore, you may have less cash on hand to pay child support than you think.

"How will I know how much support I should pay or receive?"

Each state is required by law to design guidelines by which child support is paid. A computer-generated formula calculates the amount of child support you will pay or receive. For example, I live in California. The computer program used most often in this state to calculate child support is called DissoMaster.™ Disso-Master™ is a licensed computer program published by The California Family Law Report that converts state law support requirements into an easy-to-use format. It is updated on a yearly basis.

In most states, child support awards are based on the documentation of income from both parents. To document this income, parents are asked to supply the following:

1. a completed income and expense declaration form
2. paycheck stubs for the last three months

3. income tax returns for the last two years
4. verification of earnings obtained from employer
5. income information obtained from the state employment development department

Someone who receives welfare is considered to have no income, so an income and expense declaration is not required. Each party's gross income is then determined by using one or more of the above. You will also have to supply:

- the number of children for whom child support is needed
- current tax filing status
- current dependents for whom both parties are responsible. For example, are you already paying child support for another child from a previous relationship?
- monthly or yearly gross income for both parties
- amount of visitation actually executed by the noncustodial parent

Each state's laws are different. Please check those laws in your state to verify the correct requirements.

Even though the net disposable income is determined in accordance with state law, child support is the cause of many arguments and misplaced anger toward ex-spouses.

"How does she expect me to pay that?" asked Sam Birmingham, a divorced father from Charleston, West Virginia. He was angry at his ex-wife for the amount of money he was required to pay for child support each month. They had four children, and he felt the amount was "enough for another house payment." But Mr. Birmingham's anger may be misplaced. He should be reminded the amount of child support required is not an arbitrary amount determined by his ex-wife. Everything is based on the numbers entered into that computer program.

"If an ex-spouse remarries, will their new spouse's income be taken into consideration when determining child support?"

It is not supposed to, but in reality, if the new spouse is paying many of the bills, the noncustodial parent who must pay child support may have more disposable income available for the child. Conversely, if the custodial parent remarries, their new spouse may also help with the burden of meeting expenses, and they may not need as much child support as previously calculated.

But don't panic. As a rule, courts do not generally alter the amount of child support paid based on the new spouse's salary.

"My ex-wife will not allow me to see my son. Do I still have to pay child support?"

Although you may think visitation and child support are directly related, the courts regard them as two separate issues, and unless a court order has been entered allowing child support payments to be altered or suspended, you are required to support your child. However, you may have grounds to suspend your support. Some states have laws that allow suspension of child support if you can show that your ex-spouse is willfully interfering with your lawful visitation. You immediately file a petition requesting the court examine the issue.

"My ex-husband pays me child support for our three children. What happens if he dies? How will I support the kids?"

There are a few ways to approach this: He can leave a percentage of his estate to the children in a will or living trust, or it is not uncommon to require a life insurance policy payable to the children as part of his child support obligation, and list the policy in your divorce decree. If you have specific questions about this, check with an attorney.

"I am afraid this may start a huge fight, but I need to modify my child support. What do I do?"

First, talk to your ex-spouse. The fight you anticipate may not happen. Explain why you need the modification and if he/she agrees, *get it in writing.* If you meet resistance, file a petition with the court to modify your support. To do this, simply telephone your attorney, or if you do not want to use an attorney, call the family court in the county that granted your divorce. If you don't remember what county granted the divorce, check your divorce papers.

Most states have a family court service center, where mediators, counselors, or attorneys are available to advise you of what must be done to alter your child support payments or to increase or decrease visitation rights. It is a little time-consuming but not a difficult process.

Judy Franklin of Brentwood, California, offers this solution to increasing her child support payments. "I personally had been receiving a very small amount of child support since my divorce fifteen years ago. I had always worked, and since my ex-husband and I did not use an attorney when filing for a divorce, I asked for a minimal payment to help support our daughter. As I ascended the corporate ladder, money was not an issue, so his child support payments were never increased—for fifteen years. But my mother died unexpectedly, and the shock devastated me. Unable to concentrate, I chose to leave my job and grieve quietly at home. This constituted a *change in circumstances,* and I felt it necessary to ask for an increase in my ex-husband's child support payments.

The solution we decided upon may not be the conventional

one, but it worked for us. Although I had remarried and we had
enough money to keep food on the table, since I was not working,
there was no extra for the little things teenagers need: no extra
for movies, makeup, new dresses for the Christmas dance, or a
new bathing suit for the water polo team. I knew my ex-husband
was aware of our financial situation and he would balk at increasing child support because he would think we would use it to supplement our own income, not to buy our daughter the things she
needed.

I proposed that my ex-husband continue giving me the
amount of child support he normally paid but also open up a separate bank account for our daughter. This account would have
two ATM cards, one for him, one for her. He could deposit money
directly into the account, as well as monitor the balance. I would
have absolutely nothing to do with the account. Therefore, if our
daughter needed makeup or other necessities, I wouldn't be in the
position of constantly saying, "No, we can't afford it." Plus, our
daughter would learn to plan a budget and keep track of all her
expenses.

As I thought, at first my ex-husband went a little crazy over
my suggestion. He told me he would never give me one penny
more. I explained that, if necessary, I would go to court to increase the support. His reply was based on a common misconcep-
tion. He told me that going back to court would be too expensive
for me to afford, plus any court action would take years. I pointed
out that both of those statements were erroneous. You do not
need an attorney to modify your child support, and as a rule, it
takes months, not years. When he calmed down, he realized my
bank account suggestion was a great solution for us, and he consented. He decided to open an account with $200, and each
month he deposited $200 directly into it to help with our daugh-
ter's extras.

Although we never discussed it, I think he consented to my

suggestion because he did a little research. Based on his salary, after taxes and other obligations, plugging all those numbers into the computer program that determines his child support obligation, his support payment would have been close to $500 a month. I was suggesting a total of approximately $350 per month. All the appropriate paperwork was signed, and everyone was happy."

It is important to note that, to be legally enforceable, a judge must approve all changes. But here's a wild story when a change in child support was not authorized by the courts. The outcome could have been disastrous for all concerned.

A couple on the West Coast divorced. They had two children, and the father paid child support faithfully for years. His ex remarried a man in an executive position, and finances were not of concern to them. The ex-husband began to have financial difficulties. To compensate for his inability to pay child support, he decided to offer his ex-wife, who now lived on exclusive waterfront property, an expensive dock worth even more than the total amount owed to her. Since the amount of child support paid was not critical to the children's well-being, this arrangement was accepted by the ex-wife and her new husband. Everyone shook hands and the dock was attached to the ex-wife's home, increasing its value by $30,000. A bill of sale was filed away with no reference to child support payments.

Five years went by, and no child support payments were paid because of the agreement, but the home continued to appreciate. Then the new husband filed for a divorce and he requested half the equity in the home, which included the dock. Because nothing was recorded, the ex-wife's child support became part of her second divorce property settlement!

Aside from the questionable legality of this arrangement, if it wasn't for a wise judge who saw through the craziness, everyone concerned could have been in trouble. On paper, the father had not paid child support for five years, but, in truth, the dock payments were designed to be exactly the same amount as his child support payments, so no money was exchanged each month. This fact was not listed in any paperwork, but it was explained to the judge. Although the second husband balked at the explanation, the dock was awarded to the ex-wife as her separate property.

As these parents learned, it is wise not to mix child support responsibilities with any other transaction. Child support is designed to be just that, support for the child, and although remarriage may lend to less of a need for it, it is still designated for the children. And, as this ex-wife later learned, without the help of her second husband's income, child support again became a necessity.

"What is a COLA clause?"

A COLA clause is a cost of living adjustment clause added to your divorce decree to automatically increase your child support payments based on an economic indicator, such as the consumer price index.

"What are some other reasons to modify child support payments?"

Whether you pay or receive child support, you must have a valid reason to request a change. *Changed circumstances* is usually the reason cited. There are various categories of changed circumstances. For instance:

1. *Additional financial burden.* For the recipient or custodial parent, an additional financial burden is when something unexpected happens, necessitating increased child support to meet that obligation. A good example is if your child is hurt, ill, or

because she is older and things simply cost more. Nike tennis shoes for a seven-year-old cost $35. Nike tennis shoes for a seventeen-year-old cost $150. In my case, growing older was the end of Nike tennis shoes unless we found them at a discount store.

By the same token, the noncustodial parent or person paying child support, may find a reason to reduce child support payments, for example, they have had an untimely accident and cannot work. Their child support obligation may also be reduced based on an additional financial burden.

2. *Additional income from remarriage.* If someone required to pay child support remarries and is using the new spouse's income for living expenses, the custodial parent receiving child support may petition that child support be increased based on the fact that the paying parent has more of his own money to be used for paying child support.

It is also true that if a parent receiving child support remarries and is using the new spouse's income to cover expenses previously paid for by child support, the paying parent may petition to have his/her obligation reduced.

3. *Increase in the cost of living.* Inflation and the corresponding increase in the cost of living may be grounds for an increase in child support.

4. *Increase of income.* Since child support payments are based on the combination of both parents' incomes, if either parent receives an *increase* in income, a child support modification can be requested.

5. *Decrease of income.* The same as above holds true if either parent's income is *decreased* for a valid reason.

6. *Disability.* A reduction in child support payments may be sought if the paying parent is temporarily hurt and cannot meet their child support obligations. If the injury is temporary, a temporary reduction is sought. If the injury is perma-

nent, the paying parent may petition for a permanent reduction in their child support obligation. It is also true, however,
that if the parent receiving child support is hurt and can no
longer work, the paying parent may be required to pay additional child support.

7. *Financial or medical emergencies.* If either the receiving parent
   or the paying parent has a financial or medical emergency, for
   example, a sudden loss of employment or a catastrophic accident, then either parent may request a modification in child
   support.

8. *Hardship.* In recent years, a computer program has been used
   to calculate the child support obligation, and the amount of
   money paid for child support is directly proportionate to the
   combination of both parents' incomes. Using this formula
   makes it more difficult to prove hardship. But if you can
   prove that your child support obligation causes you great financial burden, there may be a chance that your child support obligation can be reduced.

9. *Needs of the child.* If the financial needs of the child decrease,
   say, the child no longer attends private school, then the paying parent may petition the court for a reduction in their
   child support obligation. It is also true that if the child's financial needs suddenly increase, for example, special tutoring
   or braces become necessary, the court may award an increase
   in child support.

10. *Second-family obligation.* The added responsibility of a second
    family may be grounds for a child support reduction.

*"Do I have to go back to court to get my child support pay-
ments increased or decreased?"*

No one likes to go back to court, which is why I always suggest
you talk to your ex-spouse first if you want to make any changes.

Perhaps the changes can be made without a fight and can be agreed upon between the two of you, without employing the extra cost of attorneys or mediators. *But all changes should be recorded in writing, and any change in visitation or child support should be authorized by the court.* This is for your protection. Angry ex-spouses can be very unpredictable.

"What if my ex-spouse moves out of state to stop paying child support? What can I do?"

There are all sorts of laws to help you retrieve unpaid child support. The Child Support Recovery Act of 1992 made it a federal crime to go to another state to avoid paying child support, but there are specifics attached to your ability to recover funds. The act only comes into play if the unpaid amount is more than $5,000 or child support goes unpaid for more than a year. Then, a first-time offender may be fined and/or imprisoned for up to six months. A second-time offender may be imprisoned for up to two years and have their wages attached, driver's license, and other professional licenses revoked, or income tax refunds intercepted. Other punishments at the discretion of the court are the seizure of your property and hours of community service. In Maine, for example, you cannot obtain a driver's license if back child support is owed.

Because the parent required to pay child support has crossed state lines for the purpose of evading their child support obligations, it is now a federal offense. The U.S. Department of Justice has developed guidelines to enforce the Child Support Recovery Act of 1992, after all available civil and state criminal agencies have been exhausted.

The Child Support Enforcement (CSE) Program, under Title IV-D of the Social Security Act, is a combination of federal, state, and local efforts to retrieve child support from parents who are obligated to pay. Every state has a federally funded IV-D agency and is required to help you recover support for your dependent children. But programs vary. In California, child support enforcement is handled through the Family Support Division of the district attorney's office, while Washington State has chosen the Department of Social Services to handle the problem.

Recovering Back Child Support—Step-by-Step

Your first step in recovering back child support should be to talk to a caseworker from your local Child Support Enforcement office. The phone number is listed in the phone directory. Once the CSE office has screened your case, the U.S. Attorney General's office can then be sure it receives all the necessary information to move the case forward.

If you would like additional information on how to recover child support, try the Internet. The Department of Health and Human Services has an extensive Website devoted to the subject: http://www.acf.dhhs.gov/programs/cse/fct/fct.4htm.

You can:

- view basic facts related to child support
- view information on significant child support enforcement
- view the child support enforcement handbook or pamphlets on-line
- view the Office of Child Support Enforcement (OCSF) fact sheets on-line
- view state profile and descriptions of state child support programs

Locating an Absent Parent

"My child's father, whom I never married, has refused to pay child support and now has moved. What do I do to get the support I need for my child?"

Before you can obtain a court order and collect support, you must establish paternity, or someone must be proclaimed the acknowledged father (see chapter two for further explanation of an acknowledged father). If you can afford an attorney, hire one. It will make the search easier. If that is out of the question, contact your local child support enforcement agency in your county. (Try the phone book.) Officials will ask you for as much information about the alleged father as possible, so collect his last known address, social security number (which is extremely important), date of birth, driver's license number—anything to help track him down.

If that doesn't work, your next step is to call upon the government's State Parent Locator Service, or the Federal Parent Locator Service if the parent has moved out of state. The SPFS and FPLS can only be used to locate people to collect child support, so if you are trying to find someone because they owe you back alimony, these agencies can't help you. Staffers run a computer search, checking unemployment records, Department of Motor Vehicle records, income tax files, and can hopefully find the responsible parent.

"How long will this process take?"

Believe it or not, the government has established strict time frames for each step of the child support recovery process. Your IV-D agency (CSE office) is required to begin working on your case within twenty days of receipt of your application. But even strictly adhering to the rules, if your ex-spouse is hiding in order to avoid paying child support, it may take quite a while. First, he has to be found, then you must establish paternity, obtain a court order, and finally collect the support. It is a much easier process if you know where your ex lives. Since locating the paying parent takes the most time, if you know where they are and you have documentation that proves him to be your child's father, then start the ball rolling by contacting your local IV-D agency, which is usually listed in the phone book under the Department of Social Services, Human Resource Division, or under Child Support Recovery.

"What recourse do I have if I can prove my ex is misusing the child support I pay each month?"

The reason child support is paid is to help with the care and feeding of the children for which we are legally responsible, but both men and women have been known to abuse the system. You would be no more surprised to learn of an ex-wife demanding additional child support for bogus reasons than you would be surprised to hear of an ex-husband evading his child support obligations. But this, of course, does not make it right. "I have no problem paying for the things my son needs," explains a divorced father who recently found the substantial increase in his child support payments paid for a romantic weekend for his ex-wife and her new boyfriend, "but I will in no way pay for extras for my ex-wife! That's going too far!"

If you can prove misuse of child support, you should take the same approach as if you are seeking to modify your child support payments. Petition the court. The reason for the modification would be proof of misuse of child support.

Food for Thought

Bill Mitchell of Lincoln, Nebraska, offers his solution to overcoming the stress and anger he felt each month when he wrote his son's child support check. He hated to write his ex-wife's name on the *Pay to the order of* line.

"I had been lagging behind on my payments. They were never a full month late, but were sometimes up to three weeks overdue. My ex-wife drove me crazy, and I knew it really bugged her when the payments were late, so I dragged them out as long as possible. Then, I once picked up my kid and noticed his tennis shoes were really ratty, and it hit me. My ex-wife didn't have a lot of money. She was remarried, but she had another child and they were making do. It wasn't like they were going on cruises to the Caribbean with my huge child support payments. I was embarrassed by how petty I had become. Now when I write out the check, I picture my kid in my mind instead of my ex-wife and the check is much easier to write."

CHAPTER NINE

A Step-by-Step Guide to Creating Your Own Custody Solution

"When one door closes another opens; but we so often look so long and so regrettably upon the closed door, that we do not see the ones which open for us."
—ALEXANDER GRAHAM BELL

Designing our own custody solution is one of the primary ways we can make the realities of divorce a little less painful for our children. In this chapter, we will review the steps necessary to write your own custody agreement. The idea is to take a little of this, a little of that. Ask your friends what has worked for them. Consider the solutions suggested in this book. Research the possibilities. Is what you propose legal in the state in which you live? Then compile all that information and, with your ex-spouse, create a custody solution that works for your lifestyle.

"What are the benefits to designing your own custody solution?"

A judge doesn't know your life. He doesn't know how close your family is or what you have gone through to get to where you are at this moment. Although judges are wise men and women, they make their decisions based on interviews, observations, and custody evaluations. They aren't there for the day-to-day living. You and your ex know your children better than anyone else. By designing your own custody solution, you can personally tailor visitation, placement, and special outings to suit your family.

"Don't people just get a divorce and then plan their life around it?"

Some do, but this is where designing your own custody solution can help your family stay on top of the disruption divorce causes. If you know at the outset that you and your ex-spouse want to share the responsibility of raising your children, then you—not attorneys, mediators, counselors, or judges—are the best ones to plan for your life after divorce.

Before You Start

There are three prerequisites to designing your own custody solution. First, you and your ex-spouse must be on speaking terms. If you can't talk to each other, you can't parent together. Add the stresses of two houses and who knows how many lives to an inability to communicate, and you have an impossible situation. If you aren't talking, there is no way to coordinate your children's schedule or establish consistent rules at both houses. You are setting poor examples for your kids for conflict resolution. In general, it just won't work.

Poor communication between parents also makes it easy for kids to play one parent against the other. If your children think you will call the other parent to confirm permission or punishment, you will rarely hear the words, "But Mom/Dad lets us do it when we are at their house." If they know you are not talking to each other, it is certain disaster. You are setting yourself up for failure.

Second, you have educated yourself and know the basic custody laws in your state. Don't diminish your chances of getting custody or shared custody because you acted impulsively! Check out your options *before* you make any final decisions.

The third prerequisite to writing your own custody agreement is that you and your ex-spouse have decided that joint custody and/or joint physical custody is the solution for your family. To tailor your own agreement, you need the ability to suggest, discuss—and compromise. As explained in chapter three, sole custody dictates that the child live with one parent, who alone makes all the decisions for that child. The noncustodial parent is granted visitation and most likely pays child support, but interaction between parents is minimal. Sole custody may be the best solution for your family, but by its name implies that the parent with sole custody has the last word. Joint custody, on the other hand, allows you the luxury of establishing a more casual placement and visitation schedule, both parents can sign legal papers, and decisions about the child's living arrangements, vacations, schooling, etc., are made jointly. Joint physical custody takes this one step further, by ordering that the children live with each parent 50 percent of the time. This is where every life skill you have ever acquired in communication and patience is put to the test.

Finding the Information You Need

As mentioned throughout this book, much of the information needed can be found in your local phone book, and the main library in your county will most likely have an up-to-date listing of current family laws in your state. The Internet offers a wealth of knowledge with a simple push of a button. Just type in "custody" in any search engine and you will find pages and pages of organizations waiting to help you. Some charge a fee, some do not.

"Do I need an attorney?"

That is up to you. Custody of your children is only one aspect of your divorce. There are other things to consider. How you will live? What is your property settlement? If you are confused about the divorce laws in your state or if you feel you are being railroaded by your ex-spouse, then an attorney is advisable. She takes care of all the paperwork, court dates, and represents your interests in court.

If you cannot afford an attorney, there are public agencies that can point you in the right direction. Try your state or local bar associations; most areas have a legal aid society. You may find an attorney who will handle your case pro bono, meaning free of charge.

Beware. Going to court is not necessarily a sign of a good attorney. It may behoove you to find one who is a good litigator and can solve problems out of court. This saves time and money, plus anytime you go to court, the final decision is in the hands of the judge, not you and your ex-spouse.

"If we decide not to use an attorney, where do I get the correct paperwork?"

Call the family court in your county, which supplies you with all the needed paperwork. Plus many courts have counselors, mediators, or even attorneys at the courthouse, who can advise you.

Ask a Friend

Don't be afraid to check with your friends to see what they have done in a similar situation. Of course, they may not be professionals, so always check out their suggestions with an attorney or legal aid society (but they may have already done all the legwork for you).

As I wrote this book I often discussed it with friends, neighbors, and the couples who attended my lectures. One day, a friend, whom I did not know had just taken her ex-husband (who now lives in another state) back to court for additional child support, discussed her own experiences. I was surprised as I listened. In three minutes she outlined the entire procedure of returning to court, starting with "in the state of California, all you have to do is call family court services and they put you in contact with the right people." Although the state in which you live may have different divorce and custody laws, the point I am trying to make is, sometimes the answers are right under your nose!

A Step-by-Step Plan

Step 1. Agree Upon the Type of Custody

"That wasn't easy," admits Susan Shaeffer of Gilroy, California. "After hours of discussion I thought we agreed on everything. Then when we walked into court the whole thing blew up in my face."

When Susan and Danny Shaeffer agreed to joint custody, they both thought they understood what that meant in practical terms.

"I thought the kids would live with me at least some of the time," Danny says. "But as I stood in front of the judge I found out that Susan expected them to live with her full time. I felt like their occasional baby-sitter. What was the advantage to joint custody? I wanted them to live with me part of the time, too."

This is an important point. Joint physical custody does not guarantee the amount of time your kids will spend with you. It only guarantees that you have agreed to discuss decisions that affect your children's welfare. It also allows that both you and your ex-spouse can sign legal papers. Therefore, since both parents were equally qualified to accept custody, the court ordered Susan and Danny into mediation—where they worked out their placement schedule.

Step 2. Decide Upon Placement and Visitation

If joint custody is chosen, many family courts prefer that parents reach their own placement decision. Judges understand that parents know their children best of all, and if placement can be unselfishly agreed upon by the parents, the children adjust more quickly. This is where the Parenting Plan discussed in chapter two comes into play. You sit down with your soon-to-be-ex-spouse and design how the family will live from this point on. You decide where the children will live, with whom, for how long, where they will spend holidays and summers, where they will be picked up and dropped off, and in general, design your lifestyle until they reach eighteen.

"There is no way I am going to sit down with my husband and rationally hash out how long the kids will be with each of us. We can't be in the same room without starting to fight," says Marsha Lockwood, a divorced mother with four children.

One of the most important things to decide when discussing your Parenting Plan is how conflict will be addressed in the future. If you have a serious disagreement concerning the children, what is your plan of action? Would you run to the nearest attorney or would you agree to seek mediation first? In your Parenting Plan, agree upon the procedure, and list exactly how you will address problems.

Sounds too logical to you? "It was just very difficult to let go," says Susan, who now gets along well with her ex-husband. "The best thing the judge could have done for us was to order us into mediation. It helped calm my fears. I was afraid if I gave an inch, I would lose my children. With the help of Joyce, the mediator, we decided on a 80/20 split and wrote a Parenting Agreement that worked for us. With the 80/20 placement decision, the children lived with me 80 percent of the time and Danny 20 percent. It wasn't that much different from my original concept, but mediation let Danny voice his opinion, as well as explained exactly how many days the children were to be with him. Twenty percent of 365 days is 73 days. Since he works full time, that was a lot of three-day weekends."

Don and Brenda, a couple I met over the Internet, say mediation was also a good experience for them. "We found our mediator through Fathers for Equal Rights. I know you think they would be biased in favor of the father, but they don't want more rights, just equal rights for a father. The mediator was a trained psychologist certified in mediation."

"The mediator sat down with us, and we had to agree what bills were my ex-wife's and what bills were mine," says Don. "In whose hands would the house stay, and who pays? This went on for hours. We fought, argued, and name-called, all the while the mediator kept bringing us back to the important issues: custody, bills for the children, school, medical, even lifestyle. We both temporarily agreed no live-in girlfriends or boyfriends for the kids' sake."

Don adds: "Our final placement decision was joint physical

custody. Brenda fought it at first, but she had to admit I was an excellent father, and it was important to me that I continue to see the kids as often as possible. With the help of the mediator, we agreed the kids would live 50 percent of the time with me and 50 percent of the time with her."

The Specifics

If you are attempting joint custody or joint physical custody, it is advisable that you live close to each other, so that when the children travel between each home, they can continue to go to the same school, attend the same church each Sunday, maintain friendships, participate in after-school sports activities in their neighborhood, and hopefully disrupt their life as little as possible when the change is made.

Danny and Susan Shaeffer agreed their lifestyle changed dramatically with the divorce. Danny now had to consider many things that he had never thought of before. "Yeah," agrees Danny, "like child care. Leanne, our youngest, is only three. When she lives with me and I'm at work, I need a baby-sitter. That was always Susan's department. I didn't even know how to go about finding quality child care."

Susan was in an equally confusing situation. She had never worked out of the home. She was the children's primary caregiver while Danny worked a full-time job. Susan now had to find part-time work to supplement her income. Although Danny was paid well, it was a huge strain to maintain two houses on a salary that had once supported only one.

Susan admits that the 80/20 placement schedule she and Danny had agreed to was fine when the children were young. But as they grew, things would have to change. Danny lived thirty miles away, in another school district, which meant different friends, different church. Richie, their oldest son, was entering first grade the next year and expressed an interest in playing T-ball. Many of the games and some of the practices fell during the time when the boys were supposed to be with Danny, which meant Dad would spend more time in Susan's "turf" than originally anticipated.

"I guess it's just something I'm going to have to get used to," says Danny. "When Susan and I decided to divorce, we both thought our interaction with each other would be cut to a minimum. I envisioned saying hello and good-bye when we picked up and dropped off the kids. Now we understand that if we are both going to continue to be active in our children's lives, we'll have to talk to each other . . . and probably see each other all the time."

Step 3. Child Support

Most parents live together before they get a divorce. Both parties have an accurate idea of how much it costs to raise children, but when a couple with children separates, child support becomes an issue. You know who makes the most money and how much the other spouse needs to supplement their income with child support. The amount of child support to be paid should not surprise anyone.

To learn about the information needed to calculate the required amount of child support, check chapter eight, "Child Support: Payment, Collection, and Modification." If you cannot calculate the child support obligation yourself, you can also consult an attorney or the family court division of superior court in your county.

This was my solution. I live in Contra Costa County, California. The Family Court Service office in my area has a computer available to the public with the DissoMaster™ computer program fully installed. Truthfully, the computer is designed to be used by attorneys or the certified mediators who work for Family Court Services, but it is available for use. I entered all the pertinent information and the computer calculated the amount of child support required. That was it.

"When we got a divorce, my ex-husband and I just decided on an amount that sounded good. I was so desperate to end the marriage, I didn't question it," offers Leslie Blackstock, a mother of four. "But as time passed, my children grew older and as the things they needed cost more, I had no provision for a child support increase. When I needed more money, I had to petition the court to modify my child support payments."

Here lies the problem with attempting to write your own child custody agreement. Do as much research as you can to make sure you are represented properly. There are stipulations that could have prevented Leslie from having to return to court each time she needed a support modification. The best way to ensure that your rights are protected is to contact an attorney or legal aid service in your area.

Step 4. Setting In

What reads well on paper may not work as well in reality. The living of the life you design may not be what you imagined. "Everything looked good on paper," says Donald Johanssen, a newly divorced father of three, who was awarded joint physical custody of his children. "We decided the kids would be with me the first half of the month and then live with Samantha the last half, but it was difficult to get used to the practical everyday living. Samantha and I fought whenever we met, and we could never agree upon a drop-off spot that suited both of us. She would be late, then I would be angry, and Joshua, Lyle, and LeeAnne would inevitably be crying when we left.

"The rules at my home were far stricter than at Samantha's. It looked to me as if the inconsistencies from house-to-house lengthened the children's period of adjustment as they traveled back and forth. On the day the kids returned, they seemed sullen and didn't want to do anything but watch TV. When I told Sam about this, she took it personally and we got into a huge fight—in front of the kids, of course. It was terrible. Finally, one day it got so crazy, Samantha began crying from the first moment she saw me, which scared the children, and we realized that this joint physical custody thing could not work unless we took control and made it work. We would have to let go of the little things that made us crazy and work toward the finer goal of raising happy children. So Samantha and I began a series of discussions, where we compromised, even on some of the stupidest things," he notes.

Samantha and Donald set up a formal time to meet each week. Since the children switched homes on Friday afternoons after school, Sunday evenings at 7:00 was a perfect time to wind down the weekend and get ready for the week ahead. "At first, the discussions were a bartering time," Don says. "I explained that the inconsistency in our rules really bugged me, and Samantha said some of the rules seemed like prison to her. For example, she let the kids fall asleep while watching TV. I used the time to read them a story. I wanted their bedtime to be the same at each house."

Through discussion, Donald and Samantha realized that Samantha liked the children to fall asleep to the television because she was tired and wanted to rest herself. Television lulled them to sleep and she could relax on the couch after a long day at work. When Donald asked what time their bedtime was at her house, she realized there was no formal time. She put the kids to bed when she was tired, turned on the TV, and then plopped on the couch to end her day.

As gently as possible, because this was a bone of contention when they were married, Donald suggested Samantha put the kids on a schedule. He suggested she initiate a formal bedtime, 8:30, just like at his house, read the kids a story, then plop on the couch a full hour earlier than she had been ending her day. Now the kids would know their bedtime was 8:30 without exception and that rules were consistent.

Samantha agreed to the 8:30 bedtime if Donald would no

longer wash out their son's mouth with soap if he brought a bad word home from school. Eight-year-old Joshua was now testing the rules. Twice during his last stay at his dad's, he was punished for using inappropriate words at home. Joshua was horrified by the soap-in-the-mouth punishment and so was Samantha when she heard about it.

"If I agreed to make an effort to keep the bedtimes consistent, I wanted Donald to agree to call me before he stuck soap in our son's mouth," laughs Samantha. "Evidently, that was the punishment he had received when he was a kid so that's what he knew to do when he was faced with a problem. I would have rather spoken to Joshua and explained why the words were inappropriate."

Donald agreed that in the name of consistency he would discuss punishments before he implemented them.

As time passed, the 7:00 Sunday meetings changed from bartering sessions to organizational meetings. Sunday nights became the times when the two parents sat down for a half hour and made sure the other parent was aware of their child's schedule for the week. They coordinated things like Joshua's dentist appointments or LeeAnne's Brownie meeting, or that Wednesday was Back to School Night.

You may ask, if Donald and Samantha could put aside their differences and compromise so rationally after divorce, why couldn't they do this when they were married? The same thought came to my mind when I read their story and marveled at the rationality of their custody solutions.

The Turning Point

"When we were married, everything was a power struggle. Now that we are divorced, living separately but trying to raise the kids together, everything is compromise," Donald explains. But, he concedes, it was a slow process. Only after much time had passed did they realize that although their married life together was over, they still had the mutual goal of raising well-adjusted kids.

"That was the turning point," adds Samantha. "When we made the effort to put aside our differences and really look for solutions."

Until that point, their divorce was just an extension of their rocky marriage. They fought constantly and everyone was unhappy, especially their children.

Everyone finds their common ground if they have common goals. For Donald and Samantha, it took two years of fighting to realize they were still in this together, raising their kids even though they were divorced. They had to look for compromises or their children would grow up severely affected by their fighting and arguing. "If you approach your problem solving and decision making after divorce with your kids in mind, you will also find your common ground," explains Samantha. "The kids didn't want this divorce. Don and I did. Every day we live with the understanding that something we did—the divorce—hurt our children. We can't take that back. Now our goal is to make life after divorce as painless for the kids as possible."

The Glitch

It can cause problems when a new partner is added to the equation. Jealousy can rear its ugly head and ex-spouses don't understand why. "Just when I thought we were doing fine and our organizational meetings were productive, Don shows up with his new girlfriend. I couldn't understand what *she* was doing there, and I was furious," remembers Samantha.

Don explains that he was becoming serious with his new girlfriend and wanted her to see exactly how he lived. Joint custody was not to be taken lightly and if they were to marry, she would be taking on a lot of responsibilities. But in his desire to communicate all this with his girlfriend, he forgot to talk to Samantha about it. Needless to say, she was angry.

"The kids are Don's and mine. I didn't feel like I had to explain to her when our son's dentist appointment was. They weren't even married," she says.

And perhaps this is where Don could have improved his communication skills. Unless the new partner is definitely becoming part of the parenting equation, there is no reason they should be in on the decision making for the children. If they had become engaged, then Samantha should have been told. At that point Don could have expressed his desire for his new partner to occasionally attend the organizational meetings, not necessarily for input but to help plan the schedule.

Of course, Don and Samantha have worked through many of the glitches of joint custody, but like many couples who attempt this solution, it has taken a lot of hard work.

"After deciding upon a custody solution, do we just add all this information to our divorce decree?"

That's the idea. You compile all the information available to you—reading the literature, discussing it with couples that are successful, consulting an attorney or legal aid society, perhaps even talking to children who live with divorce every day—and then you design a custody agreement in conjunction with your ex-spouse that resolves your custody problems. Notice I didn't mention discussing the possibilities with your own kids. Discussing custody alternatives that *may* happen with your children will only confuse them. As mentioned in chapter one, have your ducks in a row before you meet with your kids. The more positive you are about your divorce, both mentally and emotionally, the more secure your children will feel.

Add that custody agreement to your divorce decree, and with a lot of hard work it becomes your custody solution.

"What happens when you realize the custody solution you chose is not right for your family? How do you petition for a change in custody?"

Before you change the custody and visitation plan that is in place, think it through. The key is consistency for your children, so prior to making any changes, ask yourself the following questions:

1. *What will the change mean to the emotional stability of my children?* Will the change make them less anxious in their daily lives? Will they be more relaxed or sleep better at night?
2. *Will the change make my children's life less hectic and more stable?* Will they have to change schools and make new friends because of a possible change in placement, in addition to coping with their parent's divorce?
3. *Is the request for a modification in custody truly being made with my children's best interest in mind, or am I doing this out of anger for my ex-spouse or because the current custody arrangement cramps my style?* Some soul searching will tell you the answer to this one.

Weigh all the consequences and if you still think a change is in order, your first step would be to enter a *notice of motion* to start the modification proceedings. A court date will be set and the respondent will be told they have within five days of the court-appointed hearing to respond. In their response, they will state if they agree or disagree with the modification in custody. If they agree, then the modifications are made and go into effect immediately. If they do not agree, in the states where mediation is required by the courts, mediation begins and the parents try to modify the custody agreement with the help of a court-appointed mediator. If mediation is not part of the court ordered proceedings, the parents fight it out in court.

As previously mentioned, it is a good idea to consult an attorney or legal aid society when making any changes in custody or child support. Always get changes in writing.

Fear of the Unknown—Going to Court

"The thought of going to court makes me very uncomfortable," confides Blaine Gimelli, a soon-to-be-divorced father now living in Tucson, Arizona. "I've never been to court before, not even for a speeding ticket. I have no idea what to expect and I'm afraid I won't get a fair shake."

Most of us have never appeared in court, so the thought of standing before a judge for a decision as important as the custody of our children can be extremely intimidating. Many parents harbor the fear that they will "lose" their children as a result of the divorce proceedings, which only increases their anxiety. The court system was developed to protect all of us—especially our children, and your first priority should be a safe, consistent, loving environment for your children after divorce.

Here are ten suggestions that may help you when it is your turn to take the stand:

1. *Be yourself.* You will appear less nervous and more prepared.
2. *Dress comfortably and well.* If you are a parent looking for ali-

mony and child support, don't dress down in hopes the judge will feel sorry for you and award a huge settlement. As mentioned in chapter eight, "Child Support," the amount you are awarded or must pay each month, is based on your records. The judge does not award an arbitrary figure because he likes one person more than the other. By the same token, don't overdress in hopes of impressing a judge.

3. *Be polite and courteous.* Although you may feel hostile toward your ex and his or her attorney, don't let the judge in on the secret. By no means should you lose your temper in court. It will backfire. The judge will consider your behavior when making his ruling.

4. *Just answer the questions.* Many of us volunteer too much information when we are nervous. Listen to the questions and answer with yes or no as often as you can.

5. *No matter how nervous you are do not chew gum, twist your hair, or joke around.* This is serious business, and a casual attitude will be noted by the judge.

6. *Do your homework.* Be as prepared as possible and know as much about your kid's daily lives as you can. You may think this is a strange comment. Of course, parents care about the daily lives of their children, but I will never forget a remark made to me by a stay-at-home father who was in a bitter custody battle. He feared the therapist, whose job it was to analyze his children, would be biased by his gender when suggesting placement. "I bet my ex doesn't even know what our son's best friend's name is. How can you grant custody to someone who doesn't even know the name of their kid's best friend?" In response, during her interview with the mother, the therapist asked in passing the name of her son's best friend. The mother did not know the answer.

7. *Answer questions honestly and to the best of your ability.* Speak in a clear voice. Don't try to cover things up. Even the smallest

deviance from the truth, if uncovered, will reflect poorly on your credibility.

8. *Keep your child's best interests foremost in your mind.* Put your desires aside and make your requests based on what is best for your child. Under most circumstances, it is not recommended you bring your children into court.

9. *If you choose to be represented by an attorney in court, trust your attorney's judgment.* Give them all the information you can and let them represent you to the best of their ability. That's what you are paying them for.

10. *If you don't understand something, no matter how small or insignificant it seems, ask for clarification, especially if it has to do with your child's placement and the percentage of time they will spend with you.* Judges understand that divorce is disruptive for children, and they do not like to make changes in placement after the initial decision is made. And, the big question is: Do you really want to go through this again?

CHAPTER TEN

Getting Along and Making Your Custody Solution Work

"Listening, not imitation, may be the sincerest form of flattery."

—DR. JOYCE BROTHERS

I remember the time I was eating dinner with my stepdaughter and her mother, Sharyl, when a waitress who happened to be a good friend brought both of us a glass of wine and set them down in front of us. "You guys amaze me," our friend said, shaking her head in disbelief. "This one's on me."

I knew this was a heartfelt gesture on our friend's part. I had had a conversation with her only days before, when she lost her temper with me because I told her it was possible to get along with your husband's ex-wife. "Not with my husband's ex-wife. She's a lunatic. She doesn't care what her actions do to the kids." And then she proceeded to tell me horrible stories of her stepchildren being used as pawns for revenge. I had to agree. It was a sad case, and the children were reeling.

Sharyl and I were complimented by our friend's gesture, but it also prompted a conversation about times when communication wasn't that easy. When I met my husband, Larry, he and Sharyl were attempting joint physical custody of their kids but were barely talking to each other. The kids were going back and forth every few days. Their divorce was not yet final. The property settlement was up in the air. They had been separated for more than a year, but everything was still in transition. Melanie, their eldest daughter, was having a terrible time adjusting after the divorce. Everything was a mess, and, to top it all off, Larry had decided to remarry. Everyone was overwhelmed by the confusion.

Our Own Success Story

I had consented to marry Larry, and my allegiance was to him. I listened as he complained about his ex-wife, supporting him in his anger just as any good fiancée would, but in the midst of the arguing and stress, I had the opportunity to talk to Sharyl. During phone conversations, Larry would become so incensed by what she would say that he would just hand me the phone. "Here, you talk to her," and then walked out of the room.

I can still remember the first words I heard her say. There I stood, phone in hand, with my husband's ex-wife on the other end waiting, I was sure, to bite my head off. But that's not what I heard when I said hello. Instead, in desperation she asked, "Jann, why does he hate me so much?" That question threw me. I was expecting a lunatic yelling profanities. What I heard was a woman desperately looking for help from anyone, even if it was from her ex-husband's new wife, to make some sense of what they were trying to accomplish: raising healthy, well-adjusted kids after their divorce.

Rather than continue my husband's argument, I summarized in about three or four sentences what I believed to be the answer to her question. She thanked me for my frankness and we hung up. The next time she called, she did not ask to talk to Larry but to me, and much to my husband's dismay, as we spoke I didn't find her concerns of the day so far-fetched. Then, as I spoke to Larry, rephrasing things to help him understand what she was trying to communicate, it became apparent that he did not think her current concerns were that far-fetched, either.

"Larry was so used to being angry with his ex-wife he simply couldn't hear Sharyl's point of view," explains Brenda Sass, Ph.D., a family counselor familiar with our situation. Meanwhile, we had three kids, one of whom was mine, attempting to make some sense of their lives after divorce. It became my mission to help make this a working solution.

I was lucky. I married into a situation where the main concern of the two previously married parents was the welfare of *all* the children. Larry and Sharyl were just as concerned about my daughter's adjustment as they were their own children's readjustment after their divorce.

Although there was a lot of uneasiness at first, the children were not privy to it—at least not at our house. In a relationship after divorce, you are never sure of what goes on at the other home. And even though you have the greatest intentions, it's difficult to set a good example for your children if your ex-spouse does not cooperate.

Dealing with Conflict in a Divorced Family

"A child's adjustment after divorce is directly related to how they see you handle conflict with their other parent," explains Dr. Sass. "If you search for solutions and rationally discuss problems, your children will see this and mimic your behavior in their own relationships. If you are a screamer, someone who abuses or flies off the handle in the face of a disagreement, don't be surprised when your children act as irrationally as you have. You were their role model."

I can reinforce this by sharing something from my own childhood. My father had a very bad temper. Although he got over his anger quickly and resumed his normal loving behavior, we did everything we could to not cause the initial eruption. As I grew older, I observed how this angry behavior controlled the family, and I, too, learned to "lose" my temper whenever convenient. I have since changed my behavior as an adult, but it was only after I realized my angry reactions were learned behavior and I no longer wished to deal with conflict in that manner.

"My parents never fought," explains Philip Burke, a twice-divorced father with two boys. "I suppose they had arguments, but I never saw them. I remember my mother stomping around the house when she was angry with my dad. Then they would disappear into the bedroom, I guess to talk it out, but I never saw it. I have no idea how they solved their disagreements. The only arguments I was party to while growing up was when I disagreed with my dad. But then it was a power struggle and I fought to be heard. As a married adult, I argued the same way. I yelled the loudest; therefore, I thought I had the power. Both of my marriages ended in divorce."

Could it be that our relationship with an ex-spouse is just as much a training ground as a blissful marriage to teach our children to positively deal with conflict? Like Philip Burke, most children are not privy to what goes on behind closed doors and may not see how their parents work through their problems. But your relationship with your ex is an ongoing experiment performed right in front of your children. They are watching when Mom and Dad don't agree. They probably expect it. With that in mind, it's our responsibility as divorced parents to devise a working relationship with our child's other parent in order to teach our kids how to approach problems by looking for solutions in the midst of disagreement, and, more importantly, to respect the other parent even though Mom and Dad no longer live together.

Your Working Relationship After Divorce

A good working relationship with an ex-spouse will not only serve us as parents, allowing us to be more relaxed and better able to parent, but it will also serve our children. This was verified as I watched the reaction of two young boys, both age eight, playing Little League last year.

Tyler's parents had been separated for nine months. His mother and father were at odds with each other, causing Tyler's dad to sit at the other side of the field while his mother sat in the bleachers. Tyler hit a fly ball into deep center field over the second baseman's head and began to run around the bases. The crowd went wild, but after he crossed home plate for his home run, Tyler stopped cold. First he looked to his dad, then his mom, then his dad, then his mom. Both were smiling, both were cheering, but Tyler slumped over to his teammates with tears in his eyes, a strange reaction for a child who had just hit a home run.

Justin, another eight-year-old, whose parents had been divorced for two years, was also on this baseball team. Justin's father and mother sat near each other in the bleachers. Justin's mother had just remarried and her new husband was also present. When Justin hit a home run, he knew exactly where to look for the reinforcement he needed and ran to the three people cheering him on. He gave them all high fives. His coach had to reprimand him for leaving the field! He happily ran to his teammates, who also congratulated him on his good fortune.

These two stories are a perfect illustration of how when parents interact poorly, during and after divorce, it directly affects their children. Both Tyler and Justin are products of divorce. Having been separated for only nine months, Tyler was clear that his parents were not comfortable being together. They sat yards away from each other as they watched their son's baseball game. Tyler was excited after he hit that home run, but his joy was overshadowed by the fear that if he ran to Dad for congratulations, Mom would be hurt. If he ran to Mom for congratulations, Dad would be hurt. In a split second, he was reminded that his home had been torn apart and his allegiance was split between his two parents. Because he could not choose without hurting one or the other, he did nothing. He hung his head and walked over to his teammates.

Did Tyler's parents do something deliberate to hurt him? Of course not. They simply wanted to watch their son play baseball. But seeing his parent's public, obvious disdain for each other (they sat on either side of the field) embarrassed Tyler, put him in the position where he felt he had to choose one parent over the other—even for a second—and as a result he began to cry.

Justin, on the other hand, had none of these issues. His parents had long ago resolved their hostilities for each other. They sat near each other, publicly demonstrating their mutual support for Justin. When Justin hit that home run, he had the appropriate reaction. He was elated.

Imagine yourself in your child's place. How do they see your interaction with their other parent? Is it obvious you are angry? If it is, consider how *you* would feel if you knew your parents hated each other. Would you feel anxious when they were together? Depressed? Afraid? Would you want to protect one parent from the harsh remarks of the other?

"How the heck do I establish a working relationship with my ex-wife?" asks Matthew, a tall, middle-aged father of twin boys. "When I walk into a room, she's ready to snap my head off."

As a divorce and family mediator, I can attest to most couples feeling their work is done when their divorce is final. The anger and resentment that developed while married has carried into their relationship when divorced, but they see no reason to fix it because their relationship is over. Even though children continue to be part of the scenario, most divorced parents see no reason to work on their communication. However, Matthew's predicament is a grand opportunity to explore how mediation can help divorced couples, even when reconciliation is not an option. If Matthew's ex-wife is ready to snap his head off, as he says, that's just the tip of the iceberg. There is obviously a lot of anger preventing her from calmly communicating her feelings. Mediation will allow her to explore that anger while Matthew truly listens to her point of view. Then it will be Matthew's turn to respond, all with the final goal of establishing a working relationship after divorce. If you trust the mediation process, it really works.

Make a Success of Your Divorce

I have conducted hundreds of interviews with divorced parents who are working to resolve issues of divorce. In every case where the parent's relationship progressed past the anger and pain of divorce, they put aside their personal animosities and made their decisions based on the welfare of their children, not which partner was hurt more during the marriage or for revenge. When the arguing continued for years after the divorce, it was because the parents maintained their anger, allowing it to progress past the issues of their divorce. This made it impossible to make rational decisions for their children. No wonder, when asked if they plan to marry, children of divorce often answer, "no way." The most frequently cited reason is, "I hate the fighting."

I have always found it interesting when people say they

divorced because they wanted to end the fighting. It is my experience that divorce does not eliminate fighting. On the contrary, divorce often exacerbates it.

Although divorce statistics change every year, the Bureau of Vital Statistics still indicates that slightly more than 50 percent of all first marriages end in divorce. Even more unsettling is the growing number of second or third marriages that end in divorce—up to 70 percent!

"In this country, divorce is a way of life," explains Barbara Ols, a sixth-grade elementary school teacher who sees the child casualties of divorce every day in the classroom. "At last count, almost half of my students' parents were either going through a divorce or were already divorced. I'm divorced myself, so I can relate to the initial disorientation. It's difficult to be open to learning when your parents are splitting up and your home is in an uproar. As both an educator and a divorced parent, I can see we have to figure out a way to deal successfully with this problem. So many of our nation's children are being affected."

Tips to Make It Work:
How to Get Along After Divorce
So You Can Raise Your Kids Together

The following solutions is a list I put together after lecturing, discussing, and mediating thousands of parents in how to resolve problems so they can raise their kids together after divorce. Some of the suggestions may seem like common sense, while others may seem unconventional, but the following tips have worked for former partners who have struggled to form positive working relationships with their ex-spouses, no matter what type of custody solution was chosen.

1. *Attitude is everything.* Any professional, from therapist to cler-
gyman, will tell you that the size and depth of a problem depends on how you look at it. Even Shakespeare said, "There is
nothing good nor bad. It is thinking that makes it so." Your
attitude about your divorce will control your future relationship with your ex-spouse and the way your children approach
the divorce. Roger Crawford, resiliency expert and author of
How High Can You Bounce, Turn Setbacks into Come Backs,
suggests you meet your divorce the same way you would any
other problem in your life—head-on and with a positive attitude. "Your divorce will be what you make it. Refocus yourself to view all setbacks as an opportunity for positive
change," he continues. Use this time to reflect and make the
necessary changes to continue to live your life in a positive
direction.

2. *What is your goal?* To ensure a happy life for both you and
your kids, you and your ex-spouse must *want* your relationship to run smoothly after divorce. In chapter seven, "Joint
Physical Custody," one of the panel parents, Janet Leonard,
explains that she feels she is part of a successful joint physical
custody solution because everyone involved really *wants* it
to work. That desire prompts all the decision makers, "the
parents," as the children refer to them, to make the important concessions necessary for their two households to run
smoothly in conjunction with one another.

3. *Listen.* Many of us cling to old issues from our marriage,
which prevents us from listening to what our ex-spouse is
saying right now. I have seen this in my own experience,
when my husband was so angry at his ex-wife for things he
felt she did while they were married that he still could not
hear her two years after their breakup. When he truly listened to her current concerns, he realized they were not that
unreasonable.

4. *Ask their opinion.* Here's an interesting story I can offer from personal experience. I believe the turning point in my relationship with my husband's ex-wife came when I asked her one simple question: What do you think?

Shortly after my husband's divorce was final, his ex-wife, Sharyl, had to return to work full time. Because I worked out of my home, the children were with me as the primary caregiver every other week for a full week. When Sharyl had to work late on her weeks, I filled in. Although she knew of me before her ex-husband married me, she did not know me as a person. I put myself in her shoes. I asked myself how I would feel if my daughter lived for a week at a time with a woman I didn't know well. Sure, one could say that the children were also with their father, but he was at work all day, and what ex-wife really trusts her husband's choice in a new partner? I was the one to take care of the children when they were sick, establish household rules, feed them nutritious meals, and help with homework after school. I realized Sharyl was probably concerned about the welfare of her children just as I would be were the situation reversed.

One day, my stepson, Steven, misbehaved at school and the principal called to report the situation. My husband could not be reached, and in order to preserve consistency in discipline between both houses, I called Sharyl at work and asked how she would handle the situation if Steven were at her home for the week. She was elated that someone valued her opinion. Until this time, she had felt completely left out of the loop, which caused frustration and fueled her animosity toward me and my husband. To be honest, I knew we would agree on the issue, so I was not sticking my neck out too far, but this simple act opened up a line of communication that now enables us to be friends. Because she could see I was truly concerned for her son and was trying to be consistent with the children, she also offered the same courtesy in the future, and now it is not uncommon for us to chat on a daily basis just to touch base, make sure we have the kids' schedules straight, and plan the weeks ahead.

My relationship with Sharyl has not always been easy. There were times in the beginning when we did not talk at all, which I firmly believe perpetuated the animosity we may have initially felt for each other. When we began to personally compare notes about the children, heard each other's voice on the telephone, we realized our morals and desires for the kids were the same. And when our daughter Melanie (her biological, my step) received the Most Improved Award at her eighth-grade graduation after struggling for years with reading problems, my husband was definitely the proud papa, but it was Sharyl's wink from across the room that brought a tear to my eye. That is when I knew we were just fine, and more importantly, so was Melanie.

5. *Be careful what you say.* The semantics of divorce can be troublesome to a young child, demonstrated by this story told to me by a seven-year-old girl. She explained that her parents had just separated and a friend of her mother's introduced her as coming from a "broken home." This little girl was recovering from the trauma of moving from her childhood home into a condominium with her mother. She had no idea what a broken home was. Unsure why she had to leave her home in the first place, she deduced that perhaps it was because her home was broken, just the same as if she could no longer play with her favorite toy because it was broken. She told me she was embarrassed and confused, and began to cry right in the middle of the introduction.

   Children of divorce often feel like second-class citizens. Society has told them that nuclear families are the best and since they don't live in a nuclear family, their family is not as good. Phrases like *broken home*, *failed marriage*, even *step-child*, can be hurtful and have negative connotations children do not understand.

In this book I refer to my stepchildren as "step" to easily communicate about whom I am speaking, but in everyday conversation I call them my bonus kids. It usually gets a laugh and prompts the following story.

While at an after-school basketball game with Melanie and Steven's mother, Sharyl explained that Mel did not like to call her stepfather "step" because her friends automatically thought she did not like him. This bothered Melanie because she enjoyed a lovely relationship with her stepfather and did not want to give a negative impression to her friends. In the middle of the conversation, someone behind us piped up, "Bonus. Call him your bonus dad." The friend was joking, but I liked the idea. From that day on, I have always referred to my stepkids as my bonus kids and they refer to me as their "bonus mom." A bonus is a positive, something extra, and they were definitely a positive extra to marrying their father.

6. *Guard your thoughts.* Old thought patterns can get you into trouble, as this story from a divorced mother from Sheraton, Iowa, illustrates.

"I was very unhappy when I first married my husband five years ago. He and his ex-wife shared joint physical custody of their kids and the constant bickering kept me in a terrible state. I was on the verge of leaving him myself!

"To start my day each morning, I sat down in front of my makeup mirror to put on my makeup. As I began the first step of applying the foundation, I would think of my husband's ex-wife and scream at her in my mind, telling her everything that really bugged me about her inconsistencies in discipline, her dishonesty, everything! By the time I reached my eyeliner, I was fuming.

"Then, one morning, my husband tiptoed in behind me. 'What are you doing?' I asked, not looking up from the mirror. 'I'm trying to see how much makeup you have on,' he teased. 'For some reason, the more makeup you wear, the crabbier you are with me.'

"Quite a brilliant deduction on my husband's part, don't you think? That's when the lightbulb went on. It was a conditioned response for me. As soon as I sat down in front of that makeup mirror, I started to get angry at my husband's ex-wife. Who knew how many months this had gone on? As the minutes ticked by my anger grew to the point that my attitude toward everyone in the house was affected.

"My solution? Every time I sat down at my makeup mirror I pictured my husband's smiling face and told myself how lucky I was to finally be in a happy, caring relationship. When an angry thought popped into my mind, I replaced it with a positive thought. The next time my husband snuck into the bathroom as I applied my makeup, I unknowingly smiled at him. 'Okay, what's going on?' he asked. I was too embarrassed to tell him the truth. And, I have to admit, I now have less trouble dealing with his ex-wife."

7. *Pick your fights.* Don't sweat the small stuff. If it's not a crisis, don't make it into one. This does not mean you do not confront your ex-spouse, or that you should be an ineffective parent. It means stay calm, count to ten, and analyze the situation. As Sue Smith, a divorced mother of two teenage girls, suggests, "If your daughter comes home from her father's house with magenta hair and it's washable, tell her to go wash her hair. If it's permanent, call her dad."

8. *Don't dwell on what is out of your control.* Maintaining the same rules at both houses ensures that your children will know what is expected of them. However, this is not a perfect world and sometimes ex-spouses simply do not agree. Tom

Cozzitorto of Grand Junction, Colorado, has a solution for keeping a good perspective: "You can't get angry about things you can't control. You just have to put one foot in front of the other and live your own life. My ex-wife has different rules for the kids at her house, and I used to get so angry I couldn't sleep at night. Then I realized it's out of my hands. If my friend had different rules at his house, I wouldn't be losing sleep over it. I would explain to the kids why our rules are different and to not worry about it. So that's what I did. I explained to my children why our rules are what they are, and I stopped letting it tear me up. I can't control the situation at their mother's, and unless the children's safety is a concern, I can't worry about it."

9. *Start from scratch.* I have found a common realization of many couples was the need to stop thinking of their former partner as their ex-spouse and start thinking of them as their child's other parent. This released their emotional husband/wife attachment and allowed them to make logical decisions for their children rather than purely responding emotionally to their ex-spouse. But each says this change in attitude did not occur overnight. It took years for some.

The clearest explanation of the unconscious attachments and psychological changes that must take place after divorce were volunteered by Sharon Miller of Hartford, Connecticut, a mother divorced for three years. "My biggest revelation came one afternoon when my ex-husband was picking up the kids for his time with them. We had decided my parents' home was a safe place to do the transferring. It was a place where everyone felt comfortable.

"My ex had never met my new husband and surprisingly enough everything went quite smoothly. My mother then asked my ex-husband to stay and have a cup of coffee. He agreed, and as I sat at the kitchen table with my mother and father, my ex-husband and my new husband, I marveled at how contemporary we were in our approach to this divorce.

"Then my father suggested we play cards. No one found this to be a problem and as my father dealt the cards, I chatted with both my husband and my ex-husband. As the conversation flowed and we laughed at my father's jokes, I found myself a little confused. I wasn't sure at whom I should smile. First, I laughed with my husband, then I found myself reacting the exact same way to my ex-husband. I felt incredibly guilty, almost like I was flirting, and even though we had been divorced for three years, at that moment I realized I was still very much emotionally involved with my ex-husband. Even though the fights had been furious and we divorced, in my heart, I still felt close to him. I knew then that our relationship would have to change for us to successfully raise our children together . . . and for me to go forward in life with my new husband. The first step for me was to no longer refer to him as my ex-husband. It was difficult, but the day I heard myself refer to him as my children's father, not my ex, I knew our relationship had changed to what it needed to be to raise our children together and no longer emotionally hold on to a bad marriage."

Tim Hensley, a divorced father of two children and the director of sales and marketing of a company in northern California, approaches his ex with a different take, which has worked for him. He suggests you deal with your ex-spouse as you would any business client. "My boss told me a long time ago, 'Don't come to me with a problem unless you have the solution.' I keep that in mind when I discuss things with my ex-wife. I try to stay as unemotional as possible, and when we have a problem, I go to her with a goal and a plan of attack. She's not my favorite person, but she is my children's mother. You may not like every client you have, but you do what has to be done in order to get along and cultivate a relationship that is beneficial to everyone. I'm in sales, and the final goal is to make the sale. After a divorce, the final goal is to raise well-adjusted kids, so you deal with your ex-partner with that in mind."

10. *Stress kills.* Not a particularly profound statement, but true all the same. Doctors will tell you stress contributes to high blood pressure, heart problems, and in general, makes you a less effective parent.

"Stress kills" was added to this list because when you are stressed, your concentration is not what it should be. You go through life preoccupied, acting as if you hear your kids, but you're not really listening. You don't have the ammunition you need to effectively deal with an ex-spouse, and you may fly off the handle at things that merely merit a short discussion. Control your stress and you will be better able to assess an anxiety-producing situation, like a disagreement with an ex-spouse.

Untapped Resource:
The Advantage of a Caring Stepparent

The wicked stepmother or stepfather may exist in some cases, but more often than not, the new stepparent is a caring individual who also seeks some sort of order in their life after their own devastating divorce. They may also have children they are bringing to the new marriage, and their concern for the adjustment of their kids is as strong as yours. This common concern can be a vehicle for understanding and cooperation that enables you to get past the bad feelings of your divorce to raise healthy kids in a blended family.

"There's no way I would be friends with my husband's new

wife. Are you kidding?" says a thirty-five-year-old mother of three. But a caring stepparent can be your greatest ally in raising healthy, well-adjusted children. If the new stepparent was the cause of your divorce, then that is another problem and it is understandable why it may be difficult to get past that kind of deception. But your anger toward that new stepparent won't help your children's adjustment to the divorce. Infidelity was a separate issue that was part of your marriage. This is your divorce. Your goal after divorce is to raise healthy kids, and believe it or not, the dreaded stepparent can help you do that.

How, you may ask, can your ex's new wife or husband actually benefit you? It is not uncommon for a stepparent to become a mediator between natural parents. Arguments grow heated after divorce. Even the most sensible parents lose their perspective and control. Since the stepparent is a trusted partner of at least one of the parents concerned, he can provide a voice of reason, supplying feedback that will enable the divorced parents to approach the subject more calmly.

"But this is a dangerous approach to problem solving," warns psychologist Brenda Sass, Ph.D. "If not handled correctly, the new spouse may appear to be on the side of their partner's ex, which can cause some serious questions of allegiance. A new spouse must tread lightly if this is the approach taken."

Solutions to Good Communication with an Ex

"What I do," suggests Bruce Barrett, a thirty-eight-year-old graphic designer from Norfolk, Virginia, "is ask my wife to repeat verbatim what her ex-husband said. She's so angry at him that sometimes she thinks she knows what he *means*, but it's nothing like what he *said*. So then she responds to what she thinks he meant rather than his true request. By asking her to repeat his words I am not taking sides, I am helping her to see through her anger and respond to him *now*. She knows I love her and I hate to see her worked up, so this exercise benefits us all."

"My ex-husband's wife has definitely had a positive influence on the way we settle arguments about the kids," explains Helen, a divorced mother of two, previously married to Jake, a college professor from Jacksonville, Florida. "At first, I thought, 'I'm not sure this woman is going to help me. She's his ex-wife. She probably hates me and could care less.'"

But when questioned, Alissa, Jake's second wife, explained it also benefited her when her husband and his ex-wife got along. Alissa was now living in a blended family and trying to raise her two children from a previous marriage along with Jake and Helen's two boys. Alissa wanted to put her best foot forward and set a good example of how to resolve conflict. "If Jake and Helen continued to fight, all the kids were affected, not just theirs. And I was selfish. I hated being upset all the time. Their fighting was impacting my life, too." Her solution was to "stay fair and bring solutions to the table that I thought would benefit everyone. By setting the example and helping Jake to positively deal with his ex, if I had an argument with my ex-husband, I could depend on Jake to help me keep a good perspective and offer positive suggestions," she adds. "It would be much easier for all of us to get angry right along with our spouses, but who does that serve? No one really, and certainly not the kids."

A Stepparent's Goal: Promoting Positive Relationships

Another important role stepparents play is to reinforce a positive relationship between natural parent and child. This may be difficult for a stepparent if the natural parent is estranged from the child and a new bond has been built, but children should be encouraged to stay in touch with their natural parents unless those parents have harmed the child in some way. Speaking from experience, supporting a good relationship between natural parent and child will only benefit you as a stepparent. Putting yourself in direct competition with a beloved parent inevitably backfires.

Gloria Prader of Baltimore, Maryland, offers a sweet story of her efforts to support the relationship between her new stepdaughter and the girl's natural mother. "Five months after I married my husband, his ex-wife had a birthday. Their eight-year-old daughter was at our house that week and was horrified to realize that she had forgotten to buy her mother a present. I had no idea I should have taken her out shopping for a little something, and when her mother stopped by to pick her up that morning, we had a very sad little girl on our hands. I remembered I had just bought a lipstick and matching nail polish the day before, so we quickly wrapped them up in a gift bag and my stepdaughter happily presented them to her mother as her birthday present. As her mother opened the gift bag, the smile I got from my stepdaughter made it all worth it. She *knew* I was on her side, and reinforcing the bond she had with her mother only reinforced the bond we were building."

What the Kids of Divorce Say

Three issues pop up time and time again when talking to children of divorce about their life after the break. Of course, each situation has its own special problems, but after discussing divorce with hundreds of children, the three issues that seem to plague them the most are:

- fighting and/or arguments
- the unknown
- lack of control

Childhood Memories Form Adult Realities

A child's perception of fighting or arguing is that you don't particularly like the person with whom you are fighting. Each time a
parent fights with an ex after the divorce, a child is reminded of
the fact that the two people he loves most don't particularly like
each other. Children do not like to face the fact that their parents
no longer love each other. "It's a heavy burden to carry through
life," says Ivan Walsh, a grown child of divorce. "Each time my
parents fought, my mother would rant and rave about what a terrible man my father was. When he died three years ago, I thought
her comments would stop, but whenever she is asked about him,
she still rants and raves and I still get the same, awful feeling in
the pit of my stomach whenever she starts, even though I am
thirty-one and my father is gone."

Walsh says his mother's anger toward his father after their divorce estranged him from her. "I lived with her, I loved her, but I
didn't like her much growing up. She was continually berating my
dad, no matter what he did, and after a while I couldn't take it. I
moved out as soon as I turned eighteen, and I moved closer to my
dad."

My own stepdaughter explains in my previous book, *My
Parents Are Divorced, Too*, that it doesn't matter if your parents are
divorced, when they fight it makes kids unhappy. "I hated when
my parents fought before their divorce. I thought after the divorce, their fighting would stop. It did, really, but now and then
there was a disagreement and I never got used to it."

"I'm twenty-six years old," volunteers Sarah, a woman whose parents divorced when she was two, "and I have a lot of problems dealing with conflict. Any quarrel sends me over the edge. When I hear someone fighting, even on TV, I get the same feeling as I did when I heard my parents fight as I grew up. I will do anything to avoid an argument."

Charlynn Schmeer, a counselor whose specialty is school-age children, says, "Conflict is a normal part of life. As we grow older, we settle into how we choose to deal with conflict, but we bring all our experiences to the table, and our most successful efforts may not be the most successful solutions. People like Sarah learn to deal with conflict by avoiding it at all costs, essentially, not dealing with conflict. Sarah explains this by saying as an adult she 'will do anything to avoid an argument.' She does this because of how her parents' fighting made her feel as a child, and since she hates that feeling, she steers clear of discord of any kind. Sarah has some serious work to do if she wants to have an intimate relationship with a partner as an adult, because conflict on some level is inevitable."

Fighting or being argumentative can also be learned behavior, as Ken Pry of Juneau, Alaska, explains. "I had no brothers and sisters. It was just my mom, my dad, and me. My parents fought about everything, from what socks they should wear in the morning to how you should fold a napkin. Fighting and yelling became a way of life for me." As an adult, Ken says, he screams "at the drop of a hat," and what appeared to be his lack of control frightened his wife, Molly.

"If you disagreed with Ken," says Molly, "he immediately started an argument. He would yell and scream and I would give in just to stop the fight. It was difficult enough living with my husband acting like that, but when our son, Brett, started to manifest the same behavior at seven years old, I decided to leave Ken."

The Prys went through some extensive counseling, which

eventually brought them back into a harmonious union, but not before Brett, who is now a nineteen-year-old college student, was severely affected. "I learned that if I wanted to do something my mother didn't want me to do, I just started an argument. She hated to argue and would give in. I had to learn that yelling and arguing may be a way to blow off steam but it will not supply the answers I'm looking for," Ken adds. "I also had to face the fact that my son was unruly because he was imitating me. That was a rude awakening."

As our interview closed, Brett had an interesting observation regarding parental fights and arguments. "I have never heard one of my friends say, 'My parents solved a problem last night,' but I have heard plenty of them say, 'My parents had a huge fight last night.' This tells me that fighting doesn't necessarily solve problems."

Brett has not had many "serious" relationships with members of the opposite sex, "but when I do, I have promised myself I will resolve problems through discussion, not fighting like my parents did. It made us all too unhappy."

The Unknown

"I remember as a child simply not understanding what was going on, " explains Crystal, an adult child of divorce. "I remember feeling unorganized and insignificant. All this chaos was going on around me and I was on the sidelines, watching. I never knew what was going to happen next."

Crystal's comments don't differ from those of many children of divorce, and a child's age does not seem to make a difference. Not understanding what will happen next is a common complaint of children of divorce. Children describe the separation of their parents as confusing, and say it takes quite a while to regain their balance after Mom goes one way and Dad another.

"Of course, my parents were divorced twenty-five years ago," confides Deborah Allen, a forty-year-old telephone operator from Dallas. "Joint custody was not the norm. They battled for my sister and me and eventually split us up. One of us went with my mom, and one of us with my dad. I never forgave them for that. I loved my little sister, who was my best friend. Not only did my parents split up, but they also took my best friend. I think the worst part was they didn't tell us that this was going to happen. I never knew what was going on. No one said anything. My dad left with my sister, and that was that."

As time passed, Deborah's father had difficulty taking care of a twelve-year-old daughter by himself and released custody back to his ex-wife. "But the damage had been done," she says. "Somewhere in the back of my mind I have always been a little angry with my parents for splitting up. But I was even more angry for splitting up my sister and me. Plus, I never understood why my dad took my sister and my mom took me. It was a mess a little communication could have settled, but maybe that's why they got a divorce, the old lack of communication syndrome. Maybe I've known it the entire time. I just wanted my parents to tell me. After all, they were the parents. I was just a fifteen-year-old kid."

Just listening to Deborah discuss her parents' divorce, even though it is now twenty-five years after the fact, it is obvious she still has anger issues to address. When asked if she ever discussed these issues with her parents, or a therapist, Deborah explains, "Both my parents have resigned themselves to the fact that their divorce was the other partner's fault, and it's a funny thing about lack of communication. It becomes a way of life. My parents still struggle with the same communication problems in their subsequent relationships. When I was well into adulthood and having trouble in my own marriage, I began to go to counseling.

Now I understand why I have been so angry all my life. All my parents had to do was explain things so I knew what to expect. That would have made it much easier to cope."

Deborah's comments prove that children of divorce can carry the wounds of the split all the way through life into adulthood. She believes that the best solution to a child's confusion over divorce is to simply tell them what they can expect from your decisions concerning their lives. If her parents had done this, her resentment may have been cut to a minimum.

Lack of Control

Zoe Limbowski, another adult child of divorce, describes her parents' eventual breakup. "To me, it seemed my parents were always at odds with each other. And my father was not consistent with his visitation, so I felt like I was waiting all the time—waiting for him to visit me, waiting for him to pick me up for a special occasion, waiting for my mom to get some more money from my dad so she could buy me something I needed. I always had to wait."

Zoe's mother, Myra, reinforces her daughter's desperation. "I have memories of the classic situation, the little girl who sat by the window waiting for the daddy who would never come. There were times he would show up, but they were few and far between. As a result, as Zoe grew older she learned to be a great planner. She would plan everything down to the second. She hated not knowing what was going to happen."

"Now, as an adult," Zoe adds, "I can see little things that I find almost comical, things I know are a result of my father's unpredictability. First of all, I hate to wait for anyone. Being late drives me crazy. I hate to wait in lines of any sort. Sometimes when I'm waiting in line at the bank, I start to get a little edgy and my father automatically comes to mind!"

Lori Fiddler, a sixteen-year-old high school student, has a different take on the subject of lack of control. "Sometimes I don't want to go to my dad's. Sometimes I just want to stay home and be with my friends on his weekend, but my parents get together and make all my decisions for me and I have to go. I have no control over my own life and I hate it. It makes me hate going to my dad's, plus I'm angry at my mom for making me go."

"Sounds like those parents aren't doing enough listening," suggests John Shobe, a high school therapist for the REACH (Rehabilitation Education Awareness for Community Humanitarianism) Program for high-risk kids in California.

Margaret Romiti, another counselor with REACH, reiterates Shobe's feelings. "So many high-risk kids are children of divorce, and they are articulate about their feelings. When any parent, divorced or not, does not listen to what their child is telling them, they are in danger of alienating that child and causing resentment—especially during the teenage years, when a child feels they are equipped to make their own decisions and a parent does not recognize their growing need for independence."

The Divorced-Parent Paradox

"So what am I supposed to do?" asks Trisha Marx, an adult child of divorce who is also divorced from her child's father. "I'm completely confused. I want to do the right thing, but I'm not sure what it is!"

If you listen carefully, you are sure to hear the mixed messages given to today's divorced parents. On one hand, divorced parents are told to support their children and be sensitive to their requests. After all, their children weren't the ones to decide on the divorce. They were put into that position by the parents who desired the separation. Yet divorced parents are also told not to interfere with visitation and to reinforce the other parent's desire to see their child.

Sandy Burke, formerly Fiddler, and Lori Fiddler's mother, walks a thin line. "When Lori doesn't want to go see her dad, I'm not sure what to do. Who do I support? Lori or her dad? I want to be supportive of my child, and I understand that a child's allegiance ceases to be to their parents during their teenage years, but I also see the importance of maintaining a relationship with her father. I don't want her to be thirty years old and blame me for her not having had a relationship with her dad. I carry around enough guilt about the divorce."

Professionals remind us that it is important for a child of divorce to maintain a healthy relationship with the noncustodial parent, and unless the parent has been found to be abusive, it is the obligation of the custodial parent to support the noncustodial parent's efforts to see their child. "But what if they absolutely don't want to go?" Sandy asks. "It's a battle every other weekend."

This is when the custodial parent must examine the true reasons a child does not want to visit his noncustodial parent. It's natural for teenagers to not want to disrupt their social life, and if this is the only reason for not continuing visitation, then visitation should not be interrupted. But if *any* type of abuse is suspected, then it is the obligation of the custodial parent to intercede. "I'm just plain bored when I go to my dad's," complains Lori. "He has remarried. Their lifestyle is very couple-oriented, and *they're* the couple. I feel like I'm intruding on their privacy. Besides, they practically ignore me when I'm there. All we do is sit around and read. I hate to read."

It is important for noncustodial parents to look for ways to stay current in the lives of their children. Because they don't see their kids every day, it's easy for the noncustodial parent to lose sight of what is new and interesting to their child. One week your child may like a certain band or type of music, the next week it has changed. If you don't live with your child every day, how will you know?

Following is a very sad, true story to illustrate the point. By the time Susan Kirpatrick was ten years old, her parents had been divorced for five years. Her father lived only four miles away, so it was easy for her to spend every weekend with him. You would think this kind of constant interaction would foster a closeness between father and daughter, but it did not. Susan's father never planned specific times to spend with Susan when she visited. She was just there every weekend.

Noticing his daughter was sullen and distant during their visits, Susan's father looked for a project they could work on together. A dollhouse they could construct, paint, and furnish seemed perfect. But Susan's father rarely worked on the project. Occasionally, he would get a burst of energy and demand that Susan join him for a manic three- or four-hour stretch of cutting and gluing, but still the house remained unfinished.

For Christmas, Susan's father made a personal commitment to finish the dollhouse and present it to Susan as her main gift. The irony was Susan was now twelve years old and had little use for dollhouses. Her father, so obsessed with his own life, had not realized that two years had passed since he initially purchased the dollhouse kit, and he never understood why Susan's visits dwindled to almost nothing by the time she was fourteen.

How Do You Stay Close When You Don't Live with Your Child Full Time?

If you are the noncustodial parent and you want to stay current on your children's likes and dislikes, there are a few different things you can do:

- *Listen to your kids.* Make a special effort to take note of their likes and dislikes, current activities, types of music they listen to, and the "cool" clothes they wear.
- *Plan activities before the kids arrive.* "When Travis comes to visit on his weekends," complains Frank Butler, a divorced father of a ten-year-old boy, "I spend every waking moment entertaining him. If he's not engaged in some sort of activity every second, he complains he's bored. I'm exhausted by the time he goes back to his mother's." Frank's anticipated feeling of exhaustion is common to noncustodial parents.

"I love my kids," says Jess Fong of New York, "but trying to keep them busy is a handful."

To help Frank and Jess in their predicaments, they should plan on an activity that gets their kids out and moving around. Boredom sets in when they are inactive. And don't wait for them to tell you what they want to do. Suggest things.

"My daughter, Mary," explains Matt Shoemaker, a divorced father, "is always complaining that she's bored when she visits me, but she never wants to do anything, either."

If kids are out of their environment, they don't know how to entertain themselves. It's your responsibility to make them feel like they're part of the family—not visiting. Make sure they have some of their "stuff" around. Plan activities ahead of time.

Here's a short story to demonstrate the point. Doug was a ten-year-old fifth grader. His parents had been divorced for three years and shared custody, but Doug lived primarily with his mother. His father never missed an opportunity to spend time with his son, but each meeting started off with the same question, "So Dougie, what do you want to do?" Doug never had an answer and constantly complained. In his search to make his son happy, Doug's father one day announced that they were going ice skating. Doug hated the idea. He was ten. "Ten-year-olds don't go ice skating!" he yelled. Which, of course, made his father feel terrible, but they went anyway, and Doug whined the entire time. Doug's dad rented the skates, strapped them on his son, and pushed him onto the ice. It was then that Doug realized that ice skating was a lot like Rollerblading, something he loved, and all of a sudden the idea wasn't so bad after all.

The ice skating experience allowed Doug and his dad to do something together, plus it gave them something new to talk about. Doug was surprised that his dad knew that the origin of Rollerblading was ice skating. But if Doug's dad hadn't made the arrangements on his own, he would still be allowing his ten-year-old son to suggest things they could do on their days together . . . and ten-year-old boys may not know what to do.

- *Suggest your children bring their friends with them when they visit you.* You may want to spend quality time with your child on your designated visitation days, but occasionally allowing a friend to accompany them on their visits to your home can be a good idea for a couple of reasons. First, you will be able to see the type of kids your child is attracted to, plus you will see how your child interacts with his friends.

Second, friends prevent boredom and offer a slight reprieve from constant activity. You can catch your breath. If a friend does visit along with your child, it's a good idea to have some activities planned that will help you interact with both children. Don't just allow them to play together at your home, which defeats your purpose.

Carefully choose activities such as going to the movies. Although kids love this, sitting in a movie theater means you're sitting in the dark for two hours next to the child you haven't seen in a while. You're not actively engaging your child. If you opt for the film, be sure to have a rousing conversation about the movie afterward. However, in my experience, when a child is asked "How did you like the movie?" the reply is usually "It was okay," and that's it. Don't let that response stand. Question her further!

▪ *Keep communication open between custodial and noncustodial parents so you know when your child's likes and dislikes change.* A simple "Doug doesn't like to Rollerblade anymore; he's into skateboards" may be all that is needed. Now the noncustodial parent has something new to discuss with his son, and Doug doesn't end up with new Rollerblades for Christmas when what he really wanted was a set of new wheels for his skateboard. It will also prevent feelings like, "Dad or Mom doesn't even know me. I haven't Rollerbladed in months."

Resources

Suggested Readings for Adults

Ackerman, Marc. *Does Wednesday Mean Mom's House or Dad's House?* New York: John Wiley and Sons, 1997.

Adler, Robert E. *Sharing the Children: How to Resolve Custody Problems and Get On With Your Life.* Chevy Chase, Md.: Adler and Adler Publishers, 1988.

Ahrons, Constance R. *The Good Divorce.* New York: HarperCollins, 1994.

Bartholet, Elizabeth. *Family Bonds: Adoption and the Politics of Parenting.* New York: Houghton Mifflin, 1993.

Blau, Melinda. *Families Apart.* New York: Putnam, 1993.

Burke, Phylis. *Family Values.* New York: Random House, 1993.

Defrain, John, Judy Fricke, and Julie Elmen. *On Our Own. A Single Parent's Survival Guide.* Boston: D.C. Health, 1987.

Donahue, William A. *Communication, Marital Dispute and Divorce Mediation.* Hillsdale, N.J.: Lawrence Erlbaum Associates, 1991.

Galper, Miriam. *Joint Custody and Co-Parenting.* Philadelphia: Running Press, 1980.

Greif, Geoffrey. *The Daddy Track and the Single Father.* New York: Lexington Books, 1990.

Greif, Geoffrey and Rebecca Hegar. *When Parents Kidnap: The Families Behind the Headlines.* New York: The Free Press, 1992.

Jensen, Geraldine. *How to Collect Child Support*. Stanford, Conn.: Longmeadow Press, 1991.

Leonard, Robin and Steven Elias. *Family and Divorce Law*. Berkeley, Calif.: Nolo Press, 1996.

Marston, Stephanie. *The Divorced Parent. Successful Strategies for Raising Your Children After Separation*. New York: William Morrow, 1994.

Ricci, Isolina. *Mom's House, Dad's House: Making Shared Custody Work*. New York: Collier Macmillan, 1982.

Shapiro, Robert. *Separate Houses: A Practical Guide For Divorced Parents*. New York: Fireside/Simon and Schuster, 1989.

Warshak, Richard. *The Custody Revolution*. New York: Poseidon Press, 1992.

Suggested Readings for Children

Blackstone-Ford, Jann. *My Parents Are Divorced, Too*. Washington D.C.: Magination Press, 1997.

Blume, Judy. *Letters to Judy: What Your Kids Wish They Could Tell You*. New York: Today Reader Service, 1987.

Brown, Laurene Krasney and Marc Brown. *Dinosaur Divorce*. Boston: Little, Brown, 1988.

Crown, Bonnie. *D-I-V-O-R-C-E-S Spell Discover. A Kit to Help Children Express Their Feelings About Divorce*. Pimbrough Pines, Fla.: Courageous Kids, 1992.

Ives, Sally B., David Fassler, and Michele Lash. *The Divorce Workbook: A Guide for Kids and Families*. Burlington, Vt.: Waterfront Books, 1992.

Websites

American Civil Liberties Union's Freedom Network
www.aclu.com
Information about the full spectrum of civil liberties issues, including daily news clips, ACLU resources, organized links, Act Now! and e-mail networks sign-ups.

Custody Solutions
custodysolution.com
My Website, which discusses custody solutions, new publications, a newsletter, chat, and you can e-mail me.

The Divorce Source
www.divorcesource.com
A comprehensive informational network for divorce support. Chat and bulletin boards.

The Divorce Support Page
www.divorcesupport.com
A support site for people experiencing divorce, separation, custody disputes, alimony, visitation, etc. Chat source. Divorce professionals in your area to help you.

Divorce Net
www.divorcenet.com
Advisers on divorce, support, custody, visitation, and alimony. The family law page is dedicated to helping people through the divorce process, plus the family law page offers a state-by-state listing of divorce lawyers and information about issues pertaining to divorce. Features chat and bulletin boards.

Fathers
alt.dads-rights
Rights of fathers trying to win custody of their children in court.
E-mail source.

Locate a Mediator Directory
www.mediate.com
Everything from defining mediation and guidelines to choosing
a mediator. Informational directory with links to mediator
Websites

Parent's Ear
www.parentsear.com
News clippings of lesbian, gay, bisexual child custody cases, and
related links.

Parent Soup
www.parentsoup.com
Information regarding divorce issues, including articles from professionals and others who have "been there."

United Fathers of America
fathersunited.com
Helps fathers with custody, visitation, divorce, paternity, and
child support problems.

Women Journeys—An Empowerment Place
www.womenjourneys.com
On-line magazine dealing with women's issues, including divorce
and custody.

National Organizations and Support Groups

Academy of Family Mediators
4 Militia Drive
Lexington, MA 02173
(617) 674-2663

This organization promotes mediation as an alternative to the adversarial system and publishes various periodicals, audiotapes, and videotapes.

Alliance for Divorce and Marriage Reform
3368 Governor Drive, Suite 208-F
San Diego, CA 92122
(619) 677-0505

Educates women in understanding their rights in the judicial system and working with attorneys.

American Bar Association
Section on Dispute Resolution
1800 M Street, NW, 2nd Floor, South Lobby
Washington, DC 20036
(202) 662-1680

American Bar Association
Section on Family Law
750 N. Lakeshore Drive
Chicago, IL 60611
(312) 988-5000
1-800-621-6159

American Bar Association
Standing Committee on Dispute Resolution
1800 M Street, NW, Suite 790
Washington, DC 20036
(202) 331-2258

This division of the American Bar Association provides information, services, library, and numerous publications.

American Civil Liberties Union
125 Broad Street
New York, NY 10004–2400
(212) 549-2500
1-800-775-ACLU (2258)

Publications, advocate for individual rights.

American Divorce Association of Men (ADAM)
1519 S. Arlington Heights Road
Arlington Heights, IL 60005
(708) 364-1555

This organization promotes reform in the divorce laws and encourages counseling, mediation, education, and related services. It maintains lawyer referral lists and publishes a periodic newsletter.

Association of Family and Conciliation Courts
329 Wilson
Madison, WI 53703
(608) 251-4001

This organization is composed of judges, attorneys, mediators, counselors, family court personnel, teachers and others concerned with the resolution of family disputes and its effect on children. It publishes a newsletter, directory, journal, and other documents.

Center for Dispute Settlement
1666 Connecticut Avenue, NW, Suite 501
Washington, DC 20009
(202) 265-9572

This organization promotes and evaluates mediation and similar programs, offers consulting and training, and manages a complaint center.

Children's Rights Council
200 I Street, NE
Washington, DC 20002
(202) 547-6227
1-800-787-KIDS

An organization that supports joint custody, harmony between divorced parents, and mediation, and conducts various programs and services to achieve these goals. Maintains computer databases, resource and information lists, and numerous publications for those working to promote children's rights.

Family Law Council
P.O. Box 217
Fair Lawn, NJ 07410

This organization seeks to reform current systems of divorce and supports arbitration and mediation in settling family disputes.

Fathers Are Forever
P.O. Box 4338
West Hills, CA 91308
(818) 566-3368

This organization supports parents of both genders who do not have primary custody, stepparents, grandparents, and others involved in custody, visitation, and support issues. Publishes a monthly newsletter.

Fathers for Equal Rights, Inc.
3623 Douglas Avenue
Des Moines, IA 50310
(515) 277-8789

Publishes a directory of fathers' rights organizations.

Fathers for Equal Rights (FER)
P.O. Box 010847, Flagler Station
Miami, FL 33101
(305) 895-6351

Joint Custody Association
1606 Wilkins Avenue
Los Angeles, CA 90024

Provides information on joint custody and the law.

Lesbian Mothers Resource Network
P.O. Box 21567
Seattle, WA 98111
(206) 325-2643

Mothers Without Custody
P.O. Box 27418
Houston, TX 77227
(713) 840-1622 or (815) 455-2955

Network through which mothers without primary custody of their children can share experiences. Send a self-addressed, business-size envelope with two 33-cent stamps for information.

National Center For Women and Family Law
799 Broadway, Room 402
New York, NY 10003
(212) 674-8200

National Child Support Advocacy Coalition
P.O. Box 420
Hendersonville, TN 37077
(615) 264-0151

This group advocates improved child support enforcement, changes in relevant laws, and public awareness of the effects of unpaid child support. Produces various publications and operates a referral service.

National Child Support Enforcement Association
Hall of States
400 North Capital, NW, No. 372
Washington, DC 20001
(202) 624-8180

National Coalition of Free Men
P.O. Box 129
Manhasset, NY 11030
(516) 482-6378

Advocate for legal rights of men in various legal fields, including custody. Speakers bureau, library, publications.

National Congress for Men and Children
2020 Pennsylvania Avenue, NW, Suite 277
Washington, DC 20006
(202) FATHERS
1-800-773-DADS

Provides advocacy for fathers trying to obtain or modify custody, visitation, or support orders.

National Congress For Men
11705 N. Adrian Hwy.
Clinton, MI 49236
(202) 328-4377

This coalition includes organizations and individuals promoting the rights of fathers and divorce reform. It maintains an electronic bulletin board, at (602) 840-4752, and promotes various publications.

National Court-Appointed Special Advocates Association
2722 E. Lake Avenue, E, Suite 220
Seattle, WA 98102
(206) 323-8588

This organization, composed of juvenile court judges and attorneys, advocates support programs that provide court-appointed special advocates for abused or neglected children. Produces various publications.

National Institute for Dispute Resolution
1901 L Street, NW, Suite 600
Washington, DC 20036
(202) 466-4764

National Conference of Peacemaking and Conflict Resolution
4400 University Drive
Fairfax, VA 22030
(703) 934-5141
E-mail: ncpcr@igc.apc.org

National Organization for Men
11 Park Place
New York, NY 10007
(212) 686-MALE
(212) 766-4030

This organization includes men and women who work to pro-mote equal rights of men in issues of alimony, child custody, do-mestic abuse, child abuse, and divorce.

National Organization for Women (NOW)
1000 Sixteenth Street, NW, Suite 700
Washington, DC 20036
(202) 331-0066

National Organization for Women (NOW)
Legal Defense and Educational Fund
99 Hudson Street
New York, NY 10013

This organization produces resource kits on divorce and separa-tion, child support, and child custody for $5 per kit.

National Organization of Single Mothers
P.O. Box 68
Midland, NC 28107
(704) 888-5437

National Women's Law Center
1616 P Street, NW
Washington, DC 20036
(202) 328-5160

This organization works to advance women's legal rights in areas such as child support enforcement and family law.

Organization for the Enforcement of Child Support
1712 Deer Park Road
Finksburg, MD 21048
(410) 867-1826

This group works with various branches of government to improve child support enforcement. Publications are available, including a self-help guide.

Parents Sharing Custody
420 South Beverly Drive, Suite 100
Beverly Hills, CA 90212
(310) 286-9171

Stepfamily Association of America, Inc.
215 Centennial Mall South, Suite 212
Lincoln, NE 68508
(402) 477-STEP
1-800-735-0329

Stepfamily Foundation
333 West End Avenue
New York, NY 10023
(212) 877-3244
1-800-SKY STEP

United Fathers of America
595 The City Drive, Suite 202
Orange, CA 92668
(714) 385-1002

U.S. Department of Health and Human Services
Administration for Children and Families
Office of Child Support Enforcement
370 L'Enfant Promenade, SW, 4th Floor
Washington, DC 20447
(202) 401-9373

This organization helps states develop, operate, and improve child support enforcement programs according to federal regulations.

Offices of Child Support and State Bar Associations (Listed by State)

Alabama
Alabama Office of Child Support: (205) 242-9300
Alabama State Bar Association: (205) 269-1515

Alaska
Child Support Enforcement Division: (907) 263-6279
Alaska State Bar: (907) 263-6279

Arizona
Arizona Child Support Administration: (602) 255-0236
Arizona State Bar (602) 271-4950

Arkansas
Arkansas Office of Child Support Enforcement: (501) 682-6169
Arkansas State Bar Association: (501) 375-4605

California
California Child Support, Program Management Branch:
    (916) 654-1556
California State Bar Association: (415) 561-8200

Colorado
Colorado Division of Child Support: (303) 866-5994
Colorado State Bar Association: (303) 860-1115

Connecticut
Connecticut Child Support Division: (203) 566-4429
Connecticut State Bar Association: (203) 721-0025

Delaware
Delaware Division of Child Support Enforcement:
    (302) 577-4807
Delaware State Bar Association: (302) 658-5279

District of Columbia
District of Columbia Paternity and Child Support Enforcement:
    (202) 724-5610
District of Columbia State Bar Association: (202) 737-4700

Florida
Florida Office of Child Support Enforcement: (904) 922-9522
Florida State Bar Association: (904) 561-5600

Georgia
Georgia Office of Child Support Recovery: (404) 331-5733
Georgia State Bar Association: (404) 527-8700

Hawaii
Hawaii Child Support Enforcement Agency: (808) 587-3698
Hawaii State Bar Association: (808) 537-1868

Idaho
Idaho Bureau of Child Support Enforcement: (208) 334-5711
Idaho State Bar Association: (208) 342-5711

Illinois
Illinois Child Support Enforcement Division: (217) 524-4602
Illinois State Bar Association: (217) 525-1760

Indiana
Indiana Child Support Enforcement Division: (317) 232-4894
Indiana State Bar Association: (317) 639-5465

Iowa
Iowa Child Support Recovery Unit: (515) 281-5580
Iowa State Bar Association: (515) 243-3179

Kansas
Kansas Child Support Enforcement Program: (913) 296-5206
Kansas State Bar Association: (785) 234-5696

Kentucky
Kentucky Division of Child Support Enforcement:
    (502) 564-2285
Kentucky State Bar Association: (502) 564-3795

Louisiana
Louisiana Support Enforcement Services: (504) 342-4780
Louisiana State Bar Association: (504) 566-1600

Maine
Maine Division of Support Enforcement and Recovery:
    (207) 289-2886
Maine State Bar Association: (207) 622-7523

Maryland
Maryland Child Support Enforcement Administration:
    (410) 333-3981
Maryland State Bar Association: (410) 685-7878

Massachusetts
Massachusetts Child Support Enforcement Unit: (617) 727-4200
Massachusetts State Bar Association: (617) 542-3602

Michigan
Michigan Office of Child Support: (517) 373-7570
Michigan State Bar Association: (517) 372-9030

Minnesota
Minnesota Office of Child Support: (612) 296-2499
Minnesota State Bar Association: (612) 333-1183

Mississippi
Mississippi Division of Child Support Enforcement:
   (601) 359-1031
Mississippi State Bar Association: (601) 948-4471

Missouri
Missouri Division of Child Support Enforcement: (314) 751-4301
Missouri State Bar Association: (314) 635-4128

Montana
Montana Child Support Enforcement Division: (406) 444-4614
Montana State Bar Association: (406) 442-7660

Nebraska
Nebraska Child Support Enforcement Office: (402) 471-9390
Nebraska State Bar Association: (402) 475-7079

Nevada
Nevada Child Support Enforcement Program: (702) 687-4082
Nevada State Bar Association: (702) 382-2200

New Hampshire
New Hampshire Office of Child Support Enforcement Services:
    (603) 271-4426
New Hampshire State Bar Association: (603) 224-6942

New Jersey
New Jersey Child Support and Paternity Programs:
    (609) 588-2361
New Jersey State Bar Association: (908) 249-5000

New Mexico
New Mexico Child Support Enforcement Bureau: (505) 827-7100
New Mexico State Bar Association: (505) 842-6132

New York
New York Office of Child Support Enforcement: (518) 474-9081
New York State Bar Association: (518) 463-3200 or
    1-800-867-6228

North Carolina
North Carolina Child Support Enforcement Section:
    (919) 828-0561
North Carolina State Bar Association: (919) 828-4620

North Dakota
North Dakota Child Support Enforcement Agency:
    (701) 224-3582
North Dakota State Bar Association: (701) 255-1404

Ohio
Ohio Office of Child Support Enforcement: (614) 752-6561
Ohio State Bar Association: (614) 487-2050

Oklahoma

Oklahoma Child Support Enforcement Unit: (405) 424-5871
Oklahoma State Bar Association: (405) 525-2365

Oregon

Oregon Child Support Enforcement Agency: (503) 378-5567
Oregon State Bar Association: (503) 620-0222 or 1-800-684-3763

Pennsylvania

Pennsylvania Bureau of Child Support Enforcement:
    (717) 787-3672
Pennsylvania Bar Association: (717) 238-6715

Rhode Island

Rhode Island Bureau of Family Support: (401) 277-2847
Rhode Island State Bar Association: (401) 277-2847

South Carolina

South Carolina Child Support Enforcement Division:
    (803) 737-5870
South Carolina State Bar Association: (803) 799-6633

South Dakota

South Dakota Office of Child Support Enforcement:
    (605) 773-3641
South Dakota State Bar Association: (605) 224-7554

Tennessee

Tennessee Child Support Services: (615) 741-1820
Tennessee State Bar Association: (615) 383-7421

Texas

Texas Child Support Enforcement Division: (512) 463-2181
Texas State Bar Association: (512) 463-1400

Utah
Utah Office of Recovery Services: (801) 538-4401
Utah State Bar Association: (801) 531-9077

Vermont
Vermont Office of Child Support Services: (802) 241-2319
Vermont State Bar Association: (802) 223-2020

Virginia
Virginia Division of Support Enforcement Program:
    (804) 692-2458
Virginia State Bar Association: (804) 775-0500

Washington
Washington Office of Child Support Enforcement:
    (206) 586-3520
Washington State Bar Association: (206) 727-8200

West Virginia
West Virginia Child Advocate Office: (304) 348-3780
West Virginia State Bar Association: (304) 558-2456

Wisconsin
Wisconsin Bureau of Child Support: (608) 266-9909
Wisconsin State Bar Association: (608) 257-3838

Wyoming
Wyoming Child Support Enforcement Section: (307) 777-6084
Wyoming State Bar Association: (307) 632-3737

Regional Representatives of the Office of Child Support Enforcement

This federal agency assists in enforcing child support orders, especially when the parents live in different states and the parent refusing to pay has crossed state lines.

Alabama, Florida, Georgia, Kentucky, Mississippi,
   North Carolina, Tennessee
101 Marietta Tower, Suite 821
Atlanta, GA 30323
(404) 331-5733

Alaska, Idaho, Oregon, Washington
2201 6th Avenue
Mail Stop RX 34
Seattle, WA 98121
(206) 615-2552

Arizona, California, Hawaii, Nevada
50 United Nations Plaza
Mail Stop 354
San Francisco, CA 94102
(415) 556-5176

Arkansas, Louisiana, New Mexico, Oklahoma, Texas
1200 Main Tower Building, Suite 1700
Dallas, TX 75202
(214) 767-4155

Colorado, Montana, North Dakota, South Dakota, Utah,
   Wyoming
Federal Building, Room 924
1961 Stout Street
Denver, CO 80294
(303) 844-5594

Connecticut, Maine, Massachusetts, New Hampshire, Rhode Island, Vermont
John F. Kennedy Federal Building, Room 2000
Government Center
Boston, MA 02203
(617) 565-2455

Delaware, District of Columbia, Maryland, Virginia, Pennsylvania, West Virginia
3535 Market Street, Room 5220
P.O. Box 8436
Philadelphia, PA 19101
(215) 596-1320

Illinois, Indiana, Michigan, Minnesota, Ohio, Wisconsin
105 W. Adams Street, 20th Floor
Chicago, IL 60606
(312) 353-5926

Iowa, Kansas, Missouri, Nebraska
Federal Building, Room 384
601 E. 12th Street
Kansas City, MO 64106
(816) 426-3584

New Jersey and New York
26 Federal Plaza
New York, NY 10278
(212) 264-2890

Bibliography

Ackerman, Marc J. *Does Wednesday Mean Mom's House or Dad's?*
New York: John Wiley & Sons, 1997.

"ACLU Vows to Continue Fight as Hawaii, Alaska Voters Reject
Same Sex Marriage," ACLU Freedom Network Press Release,
4 November 1998.

Berry, Dawn Bradley. *The Divorce Sourcebook.* Los Angeles: Lowell
House, 1996.

Blackstone-Ford, Jann. "Family Matters." *Working Mother.* August
1994.

———. *My Parents Are Divorced, Too.* Washington, DC:
Magination Press, 1997.

Borders, L. DiAnne, Ph.D. "Where's Daddy?" *Adoptive Families.*
Jan/Feb 1995.

Coronado, Raymond. "Lesbian Wins Right to Visit Ex-Partner's
Child." *Sacramento Bee,* 281, 15 May 1997:A15.

Friedman, James T. *The Divorce Handbook.* New York: Random
House, 1984.

Glasen, Holly. "Mothers and Others." *SN&R,* 31 July 1997:25.

Gould, Katrina I. "Volunteers Impact Children's Lives." *The
Women's Journal,* September 1997.

Herscher, Elaine. "Same Sex Marriage Suffers Setback—Alaska,
Hawaii Voters Say 'No.' *San Francisco Chronicle,* 5 November
1998.

Leonard, Robin and Stephen Elias. *Family and Divorce Law.*
Berkeley, Calif.: Nolo Press, 1996.

Myres, Sara. "Living with Children in Our Lives." *The Latest Issue: Sacramento's News Magazine for the Gay Community and its Friends* 2, no. 8 (mid-Dec 1992):10.

National Child Support Enforcement Assocation. *NNCSEA News* XXIII, no. 4 (Fall 1994).

Newman, Gary M. "Are You Getting Divorced?" *Parent's Magazine,* November 1998.

O'Neill, Anne-Marie and Joanne Fowler. "Not Going Quietly." *People Magazine,* 10 March 1997:105–6.

Ricci, Isolina. *Mom's House, Dad's House.* New York: A Fireside Book, Simon and Schuster, 1997.

Richards, Isabelle. "Divided Loyalties: Putting Love Back into Families of Divorce." *Eternelle: Celebrating Women in Mid-Life* (Winter 1997):37–39.

Taylor, John. "Divorce is Good for You."/Sherwood, Maureen. "No, It's Not" (rebuttal). *Esquire Magazine* 127, no.5 (May 1997).

Warshak, Richard, Ph.D. *The Custody Revolution: The Father Factor and the Motherhood Mystique.* New York: Poseidon Press, 1992.

Index